Contents

P9-BJN-380

Foreword

California's architectural heritage is perhaps best expressed in the stately mansions built throughout the state by the early barons of California commerce and industry. The great houses were frequently self-erected monuments to the builders' great financial success in mining, agriculture, shipping, railroads, or other mercantile pursuits. No expense was spared in obtaining the finest in materials and craftsmanship to build these great baronial mansions. The structures were the palaces and manor houses of a frontier aristocracy and were meant to serve as architectural testaments to the owners' seemingly unlimited wealth and power.

Those remarkable structures that have somehow survived the devastations of fire, earthquake, flood, and insensitive urban redevelopment (perhaps the most devastating force of all) are today's *Historic Houses of California*. These houses collectively represent a treasured heritage and rich resource. They range in architectural style and diversity from the rough-hewn simplicity of adobe ranchos and pioneer farmhouses to the outrageous ostentatiousness of some of the turn-of-the-century structures. Each was a conscious or subconscious attempt on the part of the owner/builder to formulate a statement about his own character, or to emulate a lifestyle that seemed befitting of his accomplishments and lofty position.

The early Spanish grandee painstakingly constructed the casa grande of his vast land-grant rancho to reflect the dimly remembered elegance of Granada's famous Alhambra, a structure that was in itself only a reflection of an even more elegant lifestyle in long-ago Bagdad. The contemporaries of the California grandee emulated the style of their patron's casa grande on a smaller scale in their own ranch houses and town houses, inspiring a style variously called California Spanish, or California Rancho, and eventually, Monterey Adobe. After the Yankee invasion of California in the early nineteenth century, architectural styles began to change and the most successful of the state's early farmers, ranchers, and orchardists built great Victorian mansions at the site of their agricultural endeavors or in the valley towns that seemed to sprout at their doorstep. Their grand houses were reminiscent of the substantial homes that these California pioneers remembered from Boston or St. Louis, but which were actually American copies of a French style that emulated the architectural details of the temples and villas of ancient Greece and Rome.

In the larger metropolises, the railroad, mining, and timber barons vied with each other in erecting ostentatious mansions at the most prestigious location or the most elevated prominence in town, each one seemingly more elaborate than the one that preceded it. These mansions were perhaps the culmination of the use of private homes as architectural monuments to immense personal wealth, and yet all of these great houses of the early barons were finally surpassed, and not too many years ago, when a latter-day California grandee erected a fantasy castle on a hilltop at San Simeon. The architectural style of the fantasy castle could only be described as matching the flamboyant character of its owner.

But men are mortal, great fortunes fade, and even the palaces of kings fall victim to rot and decay unless lovingly preserved from the ravages of time and the elements.

California was fortunate in that there were so many people who appreciated the rich resource of the state's wonderful old houses. A grassroots movement of historic preservation began early in California. Some of the first historic houses to be preserved in California were often those of particular significance to the state and were incorporated into the state's historical parks and monuments. To a much lesser extent, some of the early California houses were also preserved as national historic sites and monuments.

But it remained for counties, cities, neighborhood associations, and groups of private individuals to assume the task of preserving and restoring the greatest number of the state's historic houses. Often with only the most meager of means, these groups worked tirelessly, giving of their own time, money, and talents in the cause of historic preservation. The National Trust and other preservation organizations across the nation were frequently the inspiration and model for preservation approaches, but many of the most effective techniques for fund raising and restoration (such as the popular decorators' showcase) received their most widespread application here in California. In many cases, the restoration of some of the historic homes has rekindled an interest in certain almost extinct building skills and crafts and has fostered a widespread and popular interest in historic preservation. This book is intended as a directory of historic preservation across the state, but it is also a deserved recognition of the many small historical societies and preservation groups that are most responsible for the preservation and restoration of the structures described herein.

The Editors

The
North
Coast

Jenner

Fort Ross State Historic Park

When the Russians established outposts at Fort Ross and Bodega Bay early in the nineteenth century, they had more in mind than sources of wheat and other crops for their Alaskan settlements. Rich profits were to be made from sea otter pelts and trade with Spanish California; and, as President James Monroe recognized, there was the possibility of permanent colonization. Fort Ross, the larger of the settlements, was established in 1812. Behind its high palisades are several structures that date from the period or exactly replicate the original buildings.

Commandant's House
1836

Oldest is the "new " Commandant's House, built in 1836, probably by the last commandant, Alexandr Rotchev. Here, with his wife, the witty and beautiful Princess Helena Gagarin, Rotchev presided over the last years of the fort's Russian occupancy, entertaining travelers from all parts of the world with an elegance astonishing in so isolated a settlement. While the house presently contains displays of the Russian and late Victorian periods, it will eventually depict the Rotchevs' lifestyle between 1835 and 1841.

Kuskov House
1812

This two-story log building with a central outside stairway is an exact reconstruction of the first Commandant's House, built by Ivan Kuskov in 1812. The lower floor was used for storing arms and ammunition, while the Kuskov family lived on the second story. Although the original structure was still standing after the Russians left California in 1842, it apparently was demolished in the 1870s.

Call House
1867

Sheltered by a windbreak of cypresses a few yards west of Fort Ross are ranch buildings and a late-Victorian house that were part of the 15,000-acre ranch established by George W. Call in 1873. A businessman of many parts, Call had participated in the California Gold Rush and lived in South America for thirteen years before settling down to the life of a rancher in 1873. A number of rooms in Call House will be opened in 1982 to depict ranch life during the period; the garden is under restoration.

Fort Ross State Historic Park, 19005 *Coast Highway* 1, *Jenner, CA* 95450; (707) 847-3286
Hours: 10–4:30 *daily; closed Christmas, Thanksgiving and New Year's days*
Admission fee

(Courtesy of the California Department of Parks and Recreation)

Commandant's House (opposite)

Petaluma

Petaluma Adobe State Historic Park
1836–46

A huge two-story adobe house situated on a knoll overlooking Petaluma is all that remains of what was once the largest private hacienda in California. The adobe—begun in 1836—was the center of Gen. Mariano Guadalupe Vallejo's Rancho Petaluma, a tract embracing 100 square miles of rich valley grasslands that supported several thousand head of cattle, horses and sheep. Originally the building formed a complete quadrangle, roughly 200 feet by 145 feet; but the east wing and portions of the north and south faces have disappeared, leaving the U-shaped structure that stands today. The adobe's walls were laid four feet thick at the base, their small windows with heavy wooden shutters and iron grills underscoring the hacienda's secondary role as fortress.

In 1951 the state of California acquired the adobe and began a complete restoration; today the park portrays the diversity and self-sufficiency of early California ranch life. The Vallejo family quarters and some of the rancho work rooms have been refurnished with furniture and equipment of the rancho period.

Tickets purchased for the part unit are also valid, on the day of purchase, at Sonoma State Historic Park (see *Sonoma*).

Petaluma Adobe State Historic Park, 3325 Adobe Road, Petaluma, CA 94952; (707) 762-4871
Hours: 10–5 daily; closed Thanksgiving, Christmas and New Year's days
Admission fee

(Courtesy of the California Department of Parks and Recreation)

San Rafael

Ira Cook House
1879

Built by Ira W. Cook as a guest house for visitors to his estate, this gaily painted house with ornate bargeboards is an outstanding example of the Gothic Revival style. It was donated to the city in 1905 by Cook's granddaughter Louise and her husband, John Franklin Boyd, as a memorial to their two young sons. Presently it serves the Marin County Historical Society as a headquarters and museum. Japanese maples and rare exotics grace the extensive gardens.

Ira Cook House (Marin County Historical Society Museum), 1125 B Street, San Rafael, CA 94901; (415) 454-8538
Hours: 1–4 Wednesday–Sunday
Admission by donation

(Courtesy of the Marin County Historical Society)

Tiburon

Lyford House
1876

The National Audubon Society's sanctuary at Richardson Bay shelters, besides more than two hundred species of birds and harbor seals, a two-story Victorian country home with a tower, mansard roof and ornate exterior woodwork. Lyford House, built by pioneer dairy farmer Benjamin Lyford and his wife Hilarita Reed, formerly stood at Strawberry Point; in 1957 it was floated across Richardson Bay, restored and refurnished with antiques of the period 1876–1900. The society maintains the former dining room as a gallery for changing exhibitions relating to natural history and wildlife.

Lyford House, Audubon Richardson Bay Wildlife Sanctuary, 376 Greenwood Beach Road, Tiburon, CA 94920; (415) 388-2524
Hours: 1–4 Sunday and by appointment
Admission fee

(Courtesy of the National Audubon Society)

Ukiah

Sun House
1911

This serene California Craftsman–style house was the home of Grace Carpenter Hudson, a Ukiah artist who became well known in the early years of this century for her portraits of the Pomo Indians. Aware that she was witness to a vanishing way of life, Hudson devoted her forty-five-year artistic career to recording the Pomo traditional culture and environment. Selections from her work and from the ethnographic collections of her husband, Dr. John Hudson, are now displayed in Sun House, along with memorabilia of the Hudson-Carter families.

Sun House, 431 South Main Street, Ukiah,
  CA 95482; (707) 462-3370
Hours: 12–3 Wednesday–Saturday

(Courtesy of the Sun House Guild)

The
Sacramento
Valley
& Tahoe

Chico

Bidwell Mansion
1865–68

Gen. John Bidwell, the pioneer agriculturalist and philanthropist who made the second largest strike of the California Gold Rush, purchased Rancho del Arroyo Chico about 1849, and from 1865 to 1868 engaged the fashionable San Francisco architect Henry W. Cleveland to design and build this imposing twenty-six-room Italian villa. Used as a school after Mrs. Bidwell's death in 1918, the mansion became a state historic park in 1964 and has been refurnished much as the Bidwells knew it, including some original furniture and paintings. The grounds are attractively landscaped with great shade trees, broad lawns and an old-fashioned flower garden.

Bidwell Mansion, 525 The Esplanade, Chico, CA 95926; (916) 345-6144
Hours: 10–5 daily
Admission fee

(Courtesy of the California Department of Parks and Recreation.)

Lake Tahoe

Ehrman Mansion
1901–3

"Lake Tahoe's finest summer home," a Queen Anne–style mansion in stone, was designed by Bliss and Faville for the San Francisco financier Isaias W. Hellman. It was passed by marriage to the Ehrman family. Today it is a property of the state of California, maintained partly as a museum of early Lake Tahoe history and partly as a house museum illustrative of an elegant way of life that flourished on the summer estates during the early years of this century. Plans call for restoring the mansion as nearly as possible to its appearance when the Ehrmans resided there. Among the outbuildings in the park is the William Phipps Cabin, a small log cabin built in the 1860s by one of Lake Tahoe's early residents.

Ehrman Mansion, *Sugar Pine Point State Park, North Lake Tahoe*
Hours: Fourth of July–Labor Day, 10–4 daily
Admission fee

(Courtesy of the California Department of Parks and Recreation)

Lake Tahoe

Vikingsholm
1929

Hidden among pine trees on the shores of Emerald Bay is one of the most unusual summer retreats in the country. Vikingsholm, designed for Mrs. Laura Knight by the Swedish architect Lennart Palme, is a faithful adaptation of an eighth-century Norse fortress of stone construction. There is much of interest here for enthusiasts of fine craftsmanship and Scandinavian design. A sod roof, seeded with wildflowers, covers the north and south wings. The massive timbers were hand hewn. The interior and exterior carvings follow traditional themes, and the walls and ceilings in the library and morning room are painted like those found in Swedish farmhouses. A concern for authenticity governed Mrs. Knight's choice of furnishings, too. A number of them are originals, but pieces she was unable to purchase she had copied, even to the scratches.

Vikingsholm, *Emerald Bay State Park, Lake Tahoe, CA 95733; (916) 541-3030*
Hours: Fourth of July–Labor Day, 10–4 daily

(Courtesy of the California Department of Parks and Recreation)

Oroville

Judge C.F. Lott Historic Home 1856

This Gothic Revival house was built by Judge Charles Fayett Lott, a forty-niner from New Jersey, for his bride, Susan Hyer. The home remained in the Lott family until 1962. Now the house serves as a museum; it displays furniture, paintings and household objects typical of Oroville pioneer family homes between 1849 and 1910. The attractive Victorian-style garden, with a rose garden, fountains and a gazebo, incorporates what is left of the family orange orchard.

Judge C.F. Lott Historic Home, *Sank Park, 1067 Montgomery Street, Oroville CA 95965; (916) 533-7699*
Hours: January 16–November 30, 10–4:30 Friday–Tuesday; summers only, 1–4:30 Wednesday and Thursday as well
Admission fee

(Courtesy of the City of Oroville Department of Parks)

C.F. Lott Home (opposite)

Red Bluff

Kelly-Griggs House Museum 1880

Sheep rancher Sidney Allen Griggs built this handsome Italianate mansion with a hipped roof and columned front porch. On the death of his widow, in 1931, it became the home of the Kelly family; and now the house has become a museum. It has been renovated, and it is furnished with period antiques and the Pendleton collection of paintings, the wages-in-kind of a woodcarver and painter employed in the construction of San Francisco's old Palace Hotel. Of particular interest is the Ishi Room. It features some of the possessions of Ishi, who was the last of the Yahi Indians and who, after being discovered hiding in the corral of a slaughterhouse near Red Bluff in 1911, was considered to have been the "last wild Indian in North America."

Kelly-Griggs House Museum, *311 Washington Street, Red Bluff, CA 96080; (916) 527-1129*
Hours: Summer, 2–5 Thursday–Sunday; winter, 2–4 Thursday–Sunday; closed holidays
Admission by donation

(Courtesy of the Kelly-Griggs House Museum Association)

Red Bluff

Sacramento

William B. Ide Adobe State Historic Park
ca. 1850

Extensively restored by the state in the 1950s, this simple adobe was the last home of William B. Ide, leader of the Bear Flag Party of American settlers that established the short-lived California Republic at Sonoma in 1846. The house is situated at a point where the California-Oregon Trail crossed the Sacramento River. Restored outbuildings, nineteenth-century farm equipment and furnishings of the period help convey a picture of ranch life during the Ides' occupancy.

William B. Ide Adobe State Historic Park, Adobe Road, Red Bluff, CA 96080; (916) 527-5927
Hours: 11–4 daily

(Courtesy of the California Department of Parks and Recreation)

Old Governor's Mansion
1877

This resplendent Victorian Gothic frame mansion, which served as California's governor's mansion from 1903 until 1967, was built for Albert Gallatin, a local hardware merchant, by architect Nathaniel Gooden. The land it occupies was once part of John Augustus Sutter's vast holdings. In 1887 the mansion was purchased, by Joseph Steffens, whose son Lincoln was to become a prominent journalist and political philosopher. Although its selection as the residence of California's chief executives has necessitated many alterations over the years, the interior retains much of Gallatin's original decor, notably the fine "scratch" ceilings, handcrafted bronze hardware, marble fireplaces and inlaid hardwood floors. Historical furnishings, mementos and photographs convey an intimate portrait of life in the mansion under thirteen governors.

Old Governor's Mansion, Sixteenth and H Streets, Sacramento, CA 95814; (916) 445-4209
Hours: 10–5 daily
Admission fee

(Courtesy of the California Department of Parks and Recreation)

Old Governor's Mansion (opposite)

The
Wine
Country

Calistoga

Sam Brannan Cottage
ca. 1860

On the grounds of the Calistoga Museum is one of the four-room cottages built by Calistoga's founder, Sam Brannan, for his famous spa. Constructed of wood, with an ornate, "gingerbready" porch, the cottage has been restored and furnished with period antiques. The museum contains dioramas of early Calistoga, including Brannan's spa.

Sam Brannan Cottage, Calistoga Museum, 1311 Washington Street, Calistoga, CA 94515; (707) 942-5911
Hours: 10–4 Friday–Monday

(Courtesy of the Calistoga Museum)

St. Helena

Rhine House
1883

Built by Frederick Beringer, a founder of Beringer Vineyards, seventeen-room Rhine House duplicates features of his family's ancestral home in Mainz, Germany. Particularly handsome are the leaded stained-glass windows and front door, marble fireplaces and hand-carved white oak paneling imported from Germany. Occupied by the Beringer family until the 1960s, Rhine House is now the winery offices and tasting room.

Rhine House, 2000 Main Street, St. Helena, CA 94574; (707) 963-7115
Hours: 9–4:30 daily

(Courtesy of Beringer Vineyards)

Rhine House (above)

Glen Ellen

Jack London State Historic Park

Wolf House
1911–16

House of Happy Walls
1919–22

The state park preserves forty-nine acres of novelist Jack London's Beauty Ranch, the blackened shell of his home "Wolf House," destroyed by fire the night before the Londons were to move in, and the "House of Happy Walls," built by Charmian London in 1919. By the terms of Mrs. London's will, the house is now a museum of London memorabilia, including a rolltop desk and other items from his study. Much of the furniture in the house was designed by the Londons for use in Wolf House. Jack London's grave is marked by a massive boulder of red lava on a slope about a quarter of a mile north of Wolf House.

Jack London State Historic Park, Glen Ellen, CA 95442; (707) 938-5216
Hours: Museum, 10–5 daily; grounds, 8 A.M. –sunset daily; closed legal holidays
Admission fee

(Courtesy of the California Department of Parks and Recreation)

House of Happy Walls (below)

Sonoma

Sonoma State Historic Park

In 1833, sensitive to the continuing threat posed by Russia's coastal outposts at Bodega Bay and Fort Ross, the Mexican government sent its ablest young army officer north to establish settlements in the valleys of the Sonoma region. Gen. Mariano Guadaloupe Vallejo founded the town of Sonoma a year later, and many of the buildings associated with him still stand. The state of California has set aside six of them as Sonoma State Historic Park: the Blue Wing Inn, probably built during the Gold Rush; Mission San Francisco Solano (1823); the Toscano Hotel (about 1850); the Barracks (1834–41); and Vallejo's two homes, La Casa Grande (only the servants' wing remains of this structure built about 1836) and Lachryma Montis (1851–52), now known as General Vallejo's Home. Park staff members are on duty at the mission and General Vallejo's Home; tickets purchased at one park unit are valid at all the others on the day of purchase. Tickets are also valid at Petaluma Adobe State Historic Park, General Vallejo's hacienda two miles east of Petaluma (see *Petaluma*).

General Vallejo's Home
1851–52

In the years of his declining influence and prosperity, Gen. Mariano Vallejo, Sonoma's founder, and his wife Francisco Benicia Carrillo lived in this two-story Carpenter Gothic house. They built it beside a spring that inspired its name, Lachryma Montis ("Tear of the Mountain"), of planed redwood; adobe bricks were set between the walls for insulation. Multi-gabled and elaborately tricked out with scrollwork, the house featured a white marble fireplace in each room, and the interior was finished with the finest imported hardwoods. Vallejo furnished the house with crystal chandeliers, a handsome rosewood concert-grand piano and other items from Europe. Many of these possessions have been brought back to Lachryma Montis, along with a number of his personal effects.

In the gardens is the Swiss Chalet, a structure that anticipated the "prefab" with framework that was cut in Europe, shipped around the Horn, and assembled in California. Erected to store wine, fruit and other produce, its walls contain bricks that may originally have served as ballast on sailing ships. Today it is used as a museum and interpretive center for the Vallejo Home unit of Sonoma State Historic Park.

General Vallejo's Home, West Spain Street
    and Third Street West, Sonoma, CA 95476;
    (707) 938-1578
Hours: 10–5 daily; closed Thanksgiving, Christ-
    mas and New Year's days
Admission fee

(Courtesy of the California Department of Parks and Recreation)

General Vallejo's Home (opposite)

Santa Rosa

Luther Burbank House
ca. 1884

"I shall be content if, because of me, there shall be better fruits and fairer flowers," observed the horticulturalist Luther Burbank, whose experiments in plant breeding introduced so many new varieties to the world. Burbank lived in this modified Greek Revival house from 1885 until 1906 and is buried beneath a stately cedar of Lebanon in the gardens. The house is furnished as it was when Burbank and his wife, Elizabeth Waters, lived there. Also preserved on the grounds are Burbank's original greenhouse and the old carriage house.

Luther Burbank House, *Sonoma and Santa Rosa avenues, Santa Rosa, CA 95402;* (707) 545-1414
Hours: April 1–October 31, 12–4:30 Tuesday –Sunday
Admission fee

(Courtesy of the Luther Burbank Museum)

The Bay Area

San Francisco

Haas-Lilienthal House
1886

One of the finest homes in the Eastlake–Queen Anne style remaining in San Francisco, the twenty-four-room former Haas-Lilienthal residence follows the row-house plan developed locally to make the most of the city's narrow lots. The house was built by William Haas, a prosperous wholesale grocer of Bavarian birth. It passed to the Lilienthal family by marriage and was donated to the Foundation for San Francisco's Architectural Heritage in 1973. (It is now used partially as the foundation's offices.) The house is shown with many of its original furnishings. Notable are the kitchen furniture designed by Eastlake, the stencilled leather covering the hallway walls above the paneling, and the Tiffany art glass in two of the second-floor bedrooms.

Haas-Lilienthal House, 2007 Franklin Street, San Francisco, CA 94109; (415) 441-3004
Hours: 11–4:30 Sunday, 12–4 Wednesday
Admission fee

(Courtesy of the Foundation for San Francisco's Architectural Heritage)

San Francisco

Octagon House
ca. 1861

"This Octagon House was built and owned by Wm. C. McElroy and his wife Harriet S. McElroy and is intended as their privet residence," wrote the owner, a San Francisco miller, in his letter to posterity dated July 14, 1861. Discovered ninety-one years later beneath the stairs leading to the cupola, William McElroy's letter says nothing about what it was like to live in such a structure. Its shape was believed to ensure good luck and constitutional amiability and to have a beneficial effect on unborn children. These benefits and many others attributed to the octagonal shape were theorized by Orson S. Fowler, a successful nineteenth-century publisher and phrenologist. His book, A Home for All, inspired construction of some five hundred of these residences across the country; of the five built in San Francisco, only one other survives today.

Damaged in the 1906 earthquake, re-moved from its original site across the street, and remodeled in the 1950s, Octagon House now stands in an attractive period garden and serves as local head-quarters of the Colonial Dames of America. Here the Dames' collection of late-eighteenth- and early-nineteenth century furnishings are displayed.

Octagon House, 2645 Gough Street, San Francisco, CA 94123; (415) 885-9796
Hours: 1–4 on the first and second Thursday of each month
Admission by donation

(Courtesy of the National Society of Colonial Dames of America resident in the State of California)

Octagon House (opposite)

San Francisco

Schubert Hall
1905

This Baroque-style mansion, built for John D. Spreckels, Jr., a member of the pioneer sugar family, is constructed of wood and stucco and boasts some or-nate grille work. It is now the library of the California Historical Association.

Schubert Hall, 2099 Pacific Avenue, San Francisco, CA 94109; (415) 567-1848
Hours: 10–4 Wednesday–Sunday

(Courtesy of the California Historical Society)

Schubert Hall (above)

San Francisco

Whittier Mansion
1895–6

Eminent San Francisco architect Edward R. Swain designed this rather ponderous Richardson Romanesque mansion for William Frank Whittier, one of the founders of the firm that became Fuller-O'Brien Paints. Constructed of red sandstone on a steel frame, it boasts a singularly elegant interior in which only the finest materials—rare woods, silver-plated hardware, Belgian crystal—were used. The craftsmanship throughout the mansion was of a high order, especially on the hand-carved woodwork. The mansion also featured extensive and imaginative use of electricity at a time when gas lighting was still the chief means of illumination: bare light bulbs were used decoratively in the ceilings and were effective particularly in the richly hued Turkish Lounging Room. Now the headquarters of the California Historical Society, the house is furnished with appropriate period antiques, some of them from the Whittier days.

Whittier Mansion, 2090 Jackson Street, San Francisco, CA 94109; (415) 567-1848
Hours: 1–5 Wednesday, Saturday and Sunday; closed holidays

(Courtesy of the California Historical Society)

Whittier Mansion (opposite)

Mid Peninsula

Belmont

Ralston Hall
1868

The country home of financier William Chapman Ralston reflects the imagination and flair of "the man who built San Francisco." Using a modest villa purchased from Count Leonetto Cipriani as its core, Ralston constructed an opulent eighty-eight-room mansion, surrounding it with extensive outbuildings that included a Turkish bath and a bowling alley. (Of these outbuildings, only the stone car-

riage house remains.) The mansion's foyer, with its mirrors, crystal chandeliers and grand staircase, anticipated the Palm Court entrance of the old Palace Hotel in San Francisco that Ralston later built, and the ballroom, the setting of his celebrated "lavish nights," recalls the Hall of Mirrors at Versailles. Scarcely less magnificent is the dining room, where Ralston entertained as many as 120 guests. Now part of the campus of the College of Notre Dame, the mansion has been restored to much of its former elegance and furnished with late-nineteenth-century antiques. A few of Ralston's original pieces are displayed, among them his personal desk and paintings from his collection.

Ralston Hall, *Campus of the College of Notre Dame, Belmont, CA 94002; (415) 593-1601 Hours: 10–4 Monday–Friday; by appointment only Admission fee*

(Courtesy of the College of Notre Dame)

Pacifica

Sanchez Adobe Historic Site
1842–46

Francisco Sanchez, variously San Fran-, cisco's captain of the port, commandant of the presidio and several times *alcade* (mayor), during the Mexican regime, built this two-story adobe with Monterey-style porches on an 8,926-acre tract granted him by Governor Juan Alvarado. Sanchez's original building consisted of three rooms on both floors; balconies ran along the north and south sides. Gen. Edward Kirkpatrick, who became owner in 1879, added wood-framed rooms and an interior stairway.

From 1905 until the 1920s the Sanchez Adobe served as a hotel. Thereafter it was used as a home for agricultural workers, as an artichoke storage shed and as a speakeasy. Restored in 1953 by San Mateo County, the adobe now appears much as it did in Don Francisco's day, when he played host to such celebrities as Governor Alvarado, William Ralston and Gen. John C. Fremont. The house is furnished largely with nineteenth-century American antiques.

On the grounds, the foundations of an outpost of San Francisco's Mission Dolores—probably established about 1786—have been outlined in logs. Excavations show that the outpost buildings included two granaries, a priest's quarters, chapel, foreman's quarters, kitchen and storage rooms.

Sanchez Adobe Historic Site, *Linda Mar Boulevard, Pacifica, CA 94044; (415) 359-1462*
Hours: 1–5 Tuesday and Sunday; slide show first Sunday of every month
Admission by donation

(Courtesy of the San Mateo County Department of Parks and Recreation)

Redwood City

Lathrop House
1863

This imposing two-story Gothic Revival residence of many gables was built by San Mateo County's first clerk, assessor and recorder, Benjamin Gordon Lathrop. It was later the home of Civil War hero Gen. Patrick Edward Conner. Lathrop House is now operated as a museum, with a number of Civil War–era pieces among its predominantly Victorian furnishings.

Lathrop House, *627 Hamilton Street, Redwood City, CA 94604; (415) 365-5564*
Hours: 11–3 Tuesday–Friday

(Courtesy of the Redwood City Heritage Association)

San Jose

Winchester House
1884–1922

There is nothing ordinary about the Winchester House.

Born of obsessive guilt, the largest, strangest dwelling in the United States sprawls across six acres, typically mid-Victorian in feeling with its cluttered ornamentation and plethora of gables, turrets, cupolas and varied windows. Yet in every detail of its grandeur it bears the unique imprint of Sarah Winchester's beliefs and fears.

Although construction of the house did not start until 1884, its history goes back to the Civil War when Sarah Pardee met and married William Wirt Winchester, heir to the famous rifle fortune. Their only child, Annie Pardee, died within a month of birth. About fifteen years later Winchester died of tuberculosis. Sarah regarded their deaths as the vengeance of those who had been killed by Winchester firearms. She turned for advice to a Boston spiritualist who pronounced her cursed; the only way she could escape the consequences was to move west, buy a house, and continuously build on it. Should construction ever cease, Sarah would die.

Mrs. Winchester crossed the continent, purchased an old farmhouse, and built around the clock for thirty-eight consecutive years. At the direction of spirits, she created an opulent, extraordinary 160-room home; and, for all the prevalence of occult symbology and such eccentricities as stairs that lead nowhere and doors that open on blank walls, it is marked by beauty of design, materials and craftsmanship.

Despite her unremitting precautions, Sarah Winchester died in her mansion on September 5, 1922. Emptied, abandoned and vandalized for many years, the Winchester House and its extensive grounds are now almost completely restored. Period furnishings believed to be similar to those owned by Mrs. Winchester have been placed in twenty-two of the rooms.

Winchester House, 525 South Winchester Boulevard, San Jose, CA 95128; (408) 242-2000, or, for recorded information, 247-2101
Hours: By guided tour only, from 9 daily, last tour at 4:30; the last daily tour leaves at 6 from mid-June through Labor Day
Admission fee

(Courtesy of the Winchester Mystery House, Gardens and Historical Museum)

Winchester House (previous page)

Saratoga

Montalvo Center for the Arts 1912

Montalvo, Sen. James Phelan's former summer home high in the Saratoga Hills, takes its name from the early-sixteenth-century Spanish novelist Garcia Ordonez de Montalvo, whose fictitious land "close to the Terrestrial Paradise" inspired the voyages that led to the discovery of California. The house has a somewhat Spanish look; four-hundred-year-old entrance doors brought from Granada, Spain, lead to an interior characterized by high ceilings and graceful arches. A magnificent, hand-carved grand staircase leads from the entry hall to the landing with a stained-glass window depicting explorer Juan Cabrillo's ship, the San Salvador. By the terms of Senator Phelan's bequest, the house is now a center for the arts. There are artists in residence, and the art gallery features a new exhibition each month.

A visit to Montalvo would be incomplete without a stroll through the gardens, which are replete with fountains, statuary and garden temples and which reputedly were laid out by the designer of San Francisco's Golden Gate Park, John McLaren. The gardens are surrounded by a 170-acre arboretum and bird sanctuary.

Montalvo Center for the Arts, Montalvo Road, Saratoga, CA 95070; (408) 867-3586
Hours: Gallery, 1–4 Tuesday–Sunday (gallery is closed two days monthly for changing of exhibits —call for times); garden and arboretum, 8–5 daily

(Courtesy of the Montalvo Center for the Arts)

Woodside

Filoli
1916–19

Magnificently situated in the low wooded hills surrounding Crystal Springs reservoir, Filoli was designed by Willis Polk, a prominent California architect. It was built for William B. Bourn II, the founder of Greystone Winery in St. Helena and a member of the San Francisco family that owned the fabulous Empire gold mine in Grass Valley. The sixteen-acre garden was laid out by Bruce Porter with the subsequent help of Isabella Worn.

Bourn and his wife, Agnes, resided at Filoli until their deaths in 1936; in 1937 the mansion was purchased by the William P. Roths, and in 1975 Mrs. Roth donated the mansion to the National Trust for Historic Preservation.

Though predominantly Georgian in style, the brick mansion incorporates traditional Spanish elements and features of the Stuart and Georgian periods; a two-story iron porch added in 1929 imparts a French Colonial air to the northwest corner. Of the forty-three rooms, only the lower level reception and service rooms, the ballroom and the library are presently open to the public. Palatial in scale, they are partially furnished with antiques and works of art.

Filoli's gardens, which follow French and Italian Renaissance designs, were conceived as outdoor rooms of distinctive character defined by hedges. Other buildings of interest on the property are the carriage house (1917–18) and the structure named the Tea House (1920). The Bourn family cemetery overlooks the valley from a knoll southwest of Filoli.

Filoli, *Cañada Road, Woodside,* CA 94062; (415) 366-4640 *(recorded information);* 364-2880 *(office)*
Hours: *By guided tour only, at 10 and 1 Tuesday–Saturday; reservations required*
Admission fee

(*Courtesy of the National Trust for Historic Preservation in the United States and the Friends of Filoli*)

Filoli *(below & following page)*

East Bay

Fremont

Higuera Adobe
ca. 1842; restored 1978

This simple two-story adobe at the foot of Mission Peak is from an early chapter in Fremont's history. It is one of seven adobe houses known to have been built on the Rancho de Agua Caliente granted to Fulgencio Francisco Higuera in 1839; but although records associate the adobe with Juan Crisostomo Galindo, a former sergeant of quarters at the San Francisco presidio, in 1842, the building's early history is speculative. In the 1960s the adobe was largely in ruins. Meticulously restored in 1978 to its former appearance, even to the earth floor and exterior staircase, the Higuera Adobe today demonstrates the rustic lifestyle of Mexican California. The furnishings are all locally handcrafted replicas of items used during the period from 1840 to 1850.

Higuera Adobe, 47300 Rancho Higuera Road, Fremont, CA 94538; for information, call John Weed at (415) 656-3761 or Hans Larson, Ohlone College, at (415) 657-2100, ext. 246
Hours: 1–4 on the third Saturday of each month; an audiovisual show on the adobe is given

(Courtesy of the Washington Township Historical Society Mission Peak Heritage Foundation)

Fremont

Shinn Historical Park

Shinn Historical Park is the site of two buildings that link the modern East Bay to a time not so long ago when the great cattle ranches of the Spanish-Mexican period were giving way to the fruit orchards and mixed farms pioneered by Yankee settlers. Occupying a remnant of Mission San Jose's former ranch lands, the park is a relaxing and lovely place.

Shinn House
1876

A visit to this redwood ranch house built by pioneer California nurseryman James Shinn is an opportunity to see how a gentleman farmer lived during the Victorian era. The house is furnished much as it was during the last quarter of the nineteenth century. Some of the items displayed are memorabilia of the Shinn family, one of whom was Milicent Washburn Shinn, editor of the *Overland Monthly* magazine from 1882 to 1894. The old-fashioned gardens surrounding the house have a number of James Shinn's specimen trees.

Sim Cottage
ca. 1848

Although Sim Cottage is a private residence and may not be toured, it is worthwhile to walk by for a glimpse of this unusual home. The building was constructed of lumber salvaged from ships abandoned in San Francisco Bay by their crews during the Gold Rush; on the side walls, daubings presumably made by the sailors are still visible. Captain William Sim, the first Anglo owner of the land that became the Shinn Ranch, grew the first peaches in the area. The story goes that he planned to sell them for a dollar apiece, and he set his man to guard the ripening fruit; in the morning both the man and the fruit had vanished.

Shinn Historical Park, 1269 *Peralta Boulevard, Fremont, CA 94536; (415) 656-2541*
Hours: 2–4 the first Wednesday and 1–3 the third Sunday of each month
Admission by donation

(*Courtesy of the Mission Peak Heritage Foundation*)

Hayward

McConaghy Estate
1886

Built by Neil McConaghy, an Irishman who arrived in San Leandro in 1858 with but five dollars in his pocket, this Queen Anne house evokes the lifestyle of a prosperous Easy Bay farming family toward the end of the Victorian age. The exterior features a wide, covered veranda and ornate detailing; the interior is spaciously conceived, with high ceilings and an impressive stairway. Though not original to the house, the furnishings donated by local pioneer families represent the period 1886 to 1910.

The outbuildings, behind McConaghy House, include a tank house complete with windmill and a handsome carriage house surmounted by a cupola. A collection of farm wagons, carriages and old tools is displayed here; the original horse stalls are still intact, and to the rear of the building is a blacksmith's shop.

McConaghy Estate, 18701 Hesperian Boulevard, Hayward, CA 94541; (415) 278-0198 or 581-0223
Hours: 1–4 Thursday-Sunday
Admission by donation

(Courtesy of the Hayward Area Historical Society)

Benicia

Fischer-Hanlon House
1849; reconstructed 1856
Old Capitol State Historic Park

According to family tradition, the New England–style two-story frame house adjacent to Benicia's state capitol is the unburned half of the California Hotel, which Joseph Fischer, a Swiss-born butcher and quarry owner, purchased in 1856. Fischer, who moved the structure from its original site near the waterfront, converted it into a family home by adding a front porch and several rooms to the rear. Fischer also put up outbuildings in the back, including a triple-seated privy with one seat lower for the convenience of the children.

In 1968 the house, its gardens and all the original furnishings were given to the state by Fischer's three nieces, the Misses Hanlon; it is now a unit of the Old Capitol State Historic Park. As it had remained in the same family and was maintained in much the same style for 114 years, the interiors give an unusually good idea of the nineteenth-century middle-class pioneer home. The closets even contain family clothing more than a century old, including the gown worn by Joseph Fischer's wife to the opening festivities of Benicia's State Capitol in 1853.

Fischer-Hanlon House, 135 West G Street, Benicia, CA 94510; (707) 745-3385
Hours: 12–4 Saturday and Sunday; closed all holidays
Admission fee

(Courtesy of the California Department of Parks and Recreation)

Martinez

John Muir National Historic Site

John Muir House
1882

Built by John Muir's father-in-law, Dr. John Strentzel, this seventeen-room Italianate villa was the home of the great conservationist from 1890 until his death in 1914. Much of Muir's work publicizing the preservation ethic was written in the study on the second floor. Since the original furnishings were removed after his death, the National Park Service has refurnished the house in the style of the period 1906–1914. One room documents the early activities of the Sierra Club, which Muir helped to found in 1892. A film on his life and philosophy is shown on the hour at the visitor's center.

Martinez Adobe
1849

At the eastern edge of the orchards surrounding Muir's home is a two-story adobe built by Vincente Martinez, son of the original Spanish grantee of Rancho Pinole, Don Ygnacio Martinez. While part of the Muir-Strentzel ranch, it was used as a storehouse and as a residence for the ranch overseers; later Muir's daughter, Wanda, and her husband, Thomas Hanna, made it their home. Muir would often walk there to take his meals with them and play with his grandchildren. Today the ground-floor rooms are used to display photographs of the Muir family.

John Muir National Historic Site, 4202 Al-
    hambra Avenue, Martinez, CA 94553; (415)
    228-8860
Hours: 8–5 daily except Thanksgiving, Christ-
    mas and New Year's days
Admission fee

(Courtesy of the National Park Service)

Oakland

Camron-Stanford House
1876

The elegant Camron-Stanford House, situated on the banks of Lake Merritt, is the last of the area's Victorian mansions. Designed in the Italianate style for Will Camron and later owned by Josiah Stanford, brother of railroad tycoon Leland Stanford, the house served as the Oakland Museum from 1910 until 1969. Today four rooms, restored to the style of the period 1877–81 with paintings, sculpture and furnishings, give an intimate sense of well-to-do life in that era. One room is a gallery, its walls crowded with reproductions of old masters in heavy gilt frames. On the ground level an exhibit documents the techniques employed in restoring this beautiful house.

Camron-Stanford House, 1418 *Lakeside Drive, Oakland, CA 94612; (415) 836-1976*
Hours: 11–4 Wednesdays, 1–5 Sundays
Admission by donation

(Courtesy of the Camron-Stanford House Preservation Association)

Oakland

Dunsmuir House and Gardens
1899

When Joan Dunsmuir, matriarch of the Scotto-Canadian shipping and coal-mining dynasty, relinquished control of the family holdings to her two sons, Alexander Dunsmuir at last felt secure enough to marry Mrs. Josephine Wallace, his devoted mistress of some twenty years. Dunsmuir's wedding gift to Josephine was this lovely Classical Revival mansion hidden in a valley of the Oakland Hills. The thirty-seven-room house is particularly noted for its interior woodwork and a Tiffany-style glass dome above the central staircase.

The Dunsmuirs never lived in their new home. Alexander died forty-one days after the marriage ceremony and Josephine eighteen months later. The estate was purchased in 1906 by I. W. Hellman, Jr., son of the founder of the Wells Fargo Bank, and remained in his family until 1961 when it was acquired by the city of Oakland. It was during the Hellmans' ownership that John McLaren, designer of San Francisco's Golden Gate Park, laid out the gardens (now the home of the California Spring Garden show).

Also on the grounds is an elaborate carriage house, with finely paneled horse stalls and a fancy tack room, and Dinkelspiel House, built in the 1920s as a wedding gift for Florence Hellman.

Dunsmuir House and Gardens, 2960 Peralta Oaks Court, Oakland, CA 94605; (415) 562-7588
Hours: Easter–September 30, 12–4 Sunday; guided tours at 1, 2 and 3
Admission fee

(Courtesy of Dunsmuir House and Gardens, Inc.)

Walnut Creek

Shadelands Ranch Historical Museum
1902

Pioneer fruit farmer Hiram Penniman built this spacious two-story Classical Revival house nearly half a century after he settled in the Ygnacio Valley, after a spell in the California gold fields. Furnished almost entirely with the original Penniman family furniture, the interiors reflect something of the Oriental influence current at the turn of the century and show a good deal about the ranch life of the time. The Walnut Creek Historical Society's collections are housed in one room, and many pieces of ranching equipment are displayed on the grounds behind the house.

Shadelands Ranch Historical Museum, 2660 Ygnacio Valley Road, Walnut Creek, CA 94598; (415) 935-7871

Hours: 1–4 Wednesday and Sunday; closed major holidays and August

(Courtesy of the Walnut Creek Historical Society)

Shadelands Ranch (below)

The
Gold
Country

Jackson

Amador County Museum
(A. C. Brown House)
1859

Pioneer lawyer and county judge Armistead C. Brown built this Classical Revival brick house and planted the two cedars that now tower above it. The house has been Amador County's local-history museum since 1949 and contains Robert Post's working scale models of mine structures.

Amador County Museum, 225 Church Street, Jackson, CA 95642; (209) 223-2884
Hours: 10–4 daily except Tuesday
Admission fee

(Courtesy of the Amador County Museum)

Marysville

Mary M. Aaron Memorial Museum
1857

The 1857 Marysville *City Directory* listed among the new brick houses this crenellated Gothic residence with turrets and buttresses built by Warren P. Miller at a cost of $5,000. Today the house is a museum of local history (named for the mother of a previous owner); the parlor, kitchen and one upstairs bedroom have been furnished in the style of the period. A particularly attractive feature of the house is the bricked garden with Victorian wrought-iron furniture, period plantings and a fountain that formerly stood in one of the city squares.

Mary M. Aaron Memorial Museum, 704 D
   Street, Marysville, CA 95901; (916)
   743-1004
Hours: 1:30–4:30 Tuesday–Saturday; closed
   holidays and December 24–31.

(Courtesy of the Mary M. Aaron Memorial Museum)

Vacaville

Peña Adobe
ca. 1842
Mowers-Goheen Museum

The story of the Peña Adobe begins in Santa Fe, then part of Mexico, in 1841; that year, according to the families' tradition, the Juan Felipe Peñas and the Juan Manuel Vacas began the long journey to California along the Old Spanish Trail. They were granted the Rancho Los Putos, covering ten square leagues including Lagoon Valley, and there, with the help of Santa Barbara Mission–trained Indians, they built houses for their families and vaqueros. Today only the three-room Peña Adobe remains, restored to its original appearance in 1965. The adobe is situated in an attractive park offering picnic facilities, pleasant trails, and the Mowers-Goheen Museum of local history.

Peña Adobe, Peña Adobe Park, Vacaville, CA
   95688; (707) 446-6781
Hours: 8 A.M. to dusk; closed Mondays and
   Tuesdays

(Courtesy of the City of Vacaville Parks and Recreation
Department)

The
Central
Coast

Carmel

Tor House
1915–19; added to continuously until 1963

When the poet Robinson Jeffers and his wife, Una, decided to make Carmel their home rather than the West of England, they chose a wooded site above a cove that reminded them of Devonshire's rock-strewn hills and built a romantic stone home reminiscent of an English farm-house. The heart of Tor House is the small cottage completed in 1919, which Jeffers financed in part by hiring himself out to the contractor. With his new skills, he added continuously to the house until his death in 1962; it was completed by his son Donnan, who resides there today. The building's most striking feature is Hawk Tower, its massive walls five feet thick, which Jeffers built single-handedly between 1919 and 1924. One of the rooms contains the chair, table and dictionary that he used in writing most of his later work.

Tor House, 26304 Ocean View, Carmel, CA 93921; (408) 624-1813
Hours: 10–4 Saturdays and Sundays. By advance reservation only; telephone (408) 624-1813 or write Tor House Foundation, Box 1887, Carmel, CA 93921
Admission fee

(Courtesy of the Tor House Foundation)

Monterey

Casa Amesti
1834–53

Built for the family of Don Jose Amesti, a Spanish-born merchant and landowner from San Sebastian, La Casa Amesti is an elegantly proportioned two-story adobe in the Monterey Colonial style. The original two-room structure was enlarged in 1845 and completed in 1855, shortly before Don Jose died. Little is known of its history after the Amestis departed in 1883, but in 1918 the adobe was purchased by Frances and Felton Elkins. Mrs. Elkins, a well-known interior decorator, restored the house with the assistance of her brother David Adler, the Chicago architect, who added the solarium at the rear. The formal garden with raked gravel walks and topiary work is a replica of a garden they had known and loved in Spain.

Mrs. Elkins bequeathed the adobe and its contents to the National Trust for Historic Preservation in 1954. The furnishings, an eclectic but harmonious assemblage of European antiques acquired by Mrs. Elkins, include Wedgwood busts in basalt and a rare English hunting table.

Casa Amesti, 516 Polk Street, Monterey, CA 93940; (408) 372-2608
Hours: 2–4 Saturday and Sunday. Closed Christmas Day
Admission fee

(Courtesy of the National Trust for Historic Preservation in the United States)

Casa Amesti (opposite)

Monterey

Monterey State Historic Park

Monterey, a former capital of California under Spanish and Mexican rule, is a city that cherishes its past and hospitably opens the doors of many early buildings to its visitors. The state of California preserves nine as Monterey State Historic Park; for information on those other than the homes described here, pick up a copy of the state's brochure from the park headquarters at 210 Olivier Street; (408) 649-2836. The building is open from 9:00 to 5:00 daily. Another useful adjunct to a visit to Monterey is the Old Monterey Council's brochure describing one-hour walking tours, available from information desks around the town. This points the way to all Monterey's historic sites, including many fine old homes that may be viewed from a respectful distance but not toured.

Casa Soberanes
1830

A towering hedge of Monterey cypress and an old-fashioned garden bordered with abalone shells hold time and the Casa Soberanes aloof from Monterey's busy Pacific Street. Built in the 1830s by Jose Rafael Estrada, descendant of one of the Spanish soldiery that opened California for settlement in 1769, the two-story house is considered one of the purest examples of the era's Monterey adobe architecture; it has never been altered, and it has been maintained with great sensitivity for its original construction.

Estrada built solidly in the California style. Three-foot-thick adobe walls, pierced by redwood beams that are cantilevers supporting front and rear balconies, are surmounted by lighter, narrower walls acting as cross braces. Such modernities as wooden floors, electricity, plumbing and heating were not installed until its restoration in the 1920s and 1930s. The unpretentious furnishings are largely the collection of Mrs. Mayo Hayes O'Donnell, who donated them with the house to the state in 1922. They include some forty works in various media by local artists. One room contains photographs of the casa's occupants and of the house before its restoration, which have been printed from old negatives recently discovered in the attic.

Casa Soberanes, 336 Pacific Street, Monterey, CA 93940; (408) 649-2836
Hours: 10–5 daily
Admission fee

Larkin House
1835

Located at the corner of Jefferson Street and the Calle Principal in Monterey is one of the most widely copied houses in the history of California architecture. By devising a wood frame able to support a second story of adobe and introducing the hip roof, double veranda and interior fireplace, Thomas Oliver Larkin, a Yankee merchant from Massachusetts, departed radically from traditional Spanish building techniques and set the pattern for the "Monterey" style. The house served as the consulate when Larkin was appointed the United States' first and only consul to Mexican California, from 1843 to 1846. Among the fine antique furnishings are many original Larkin items.

Larkin House, Jefferson Street and Calle Principal, Monterey, CA 93940; (408) 649 2836
Hours: 10–5 daily
Admission fee

Stevenson House
ca. 1830

The oldest portion of this two-story adobe was the home of Alta (Northern) California's first customs administrator, Don Rafael Gonzales. In 1856 Juan Girardin, a pioneer French resident, and his wife Manuela purchased the building, added the wooden section and began renting spare rooms to boarders. One was the young Robert Louis Stevenson. The writer came to Monterey in the fall of 1879 to be near his future wife, Fanny Osbourne; he occupied a second-floor room in the adobe, and he subsisted on the two dollars a week he received for articles published by the local newspapers. The house has been restored and refurnished to reflect differing periods in its history, with several rooms devoted to Stevenson memorabilia. Among them are the Chippendale desk at which he wrote part of *Treasure Island* and items from the Stevenson family home in Edinburgh.

Stevenson House, 530 Houston Street, Monterey, CA 93940; (408) 649-2836
Hours: 9–4 daily except Wednesdays

(Courtesy of the California Department of Parks and Recreation)

Salinas

Boronda Adobe
1844–48

Originally just a single room, this unpretentious Monterey Colonial adobe was built by Jose Eusebio Boronda on the 6,700-acre rancho granted him by the Mexican government in 1840. It embodies several features of Thomas Oliver Larkin's widely copied home in Monterey—a wood-shingled roof sloping in four directions; a broad, open veranda encircling the house; wood window and door sashes; and two indoor fireplaces with carved wood mantelpieces. Eusebio fathered fourteen children, so he modified the home with wooden partitions to define a bedroom, a *sala* (parlor) and an eating area, and he boarded in the side porches to create additional space.

In 1975 the home was restored to its original state with handmade materials, and it is now maintained by the Monterey Historical Society as an unmodified family residence of the Mexican period.

Boronda Adobe, *Boronda Road at West Laurel Drive, Salinas, CA 93901; (408) 757-8085 Hours: 1–4 Saturday and Sunday, and by appointment*

(Courtesy of the Monterey County Historical Society)

Salinas

Harvey-Baker House
1868

Isaac Julian Harvey, first mayor of Salinas, hauled redwood planks all the way from the early port of Moss Landing to construct this two-story frame house. Originally situated behind his general merchandise store on Gabilan Street, the house was moved to a larger lot on Monterey Street to provide room for gardens and outbuildings. In 1939 it was moved yet again, to its present location. Although currently undergoing restoration, the Harvey House remains substantially unaltered and contains the original family furnishings.

Harvey-Baker House, 238 East Romie Lane, Salinas, CA 93912; (408) 757-8085
Hours: 1–4 the first Sunday of each month, and by appointment

(Courtesy of the Monterey County Historical Society)

Salinas

Steinbeck House
1897

John Steinbeck, Pulitzer and Nobel prize winner, was born in this fifteen-room Victorian frame house on February 27, 1902. He wrote his first two novels here and, in *East of Eden*, recalled it affectionately as "an immaculate and friendly house, grand enough but not pretentious," with "roses and cotoneasters lapping against its walls." In 1973 the house was purchased by the Valley Guild, which operates it as a luncheon restaurant and uses the profits for the maintenance of the house, as well as for Salinas Valley charities. Steinbeck memorabilia is displayed in the house, and tours are conducted for luncheon patrons.

Steinbeck House, 132 Central Avenue, Salinas, CA 93901; (408) 424-2735
Hours: Tours are given restaurant guests only. The restaurant is open Monday–Friday; sittings at 11:45 and 1:15 by reservation only

(Courtesy of the Valley Guild)

San Juan Bautista

San Juan Bautista State Historic Park

Grouped around the plaza of the old mission town of San Juan Bautista are several buildings of historic interest, six of which form San Juan Bautista State Historic Park. They are the Plaza Hotel, incorporating the original Spanish barracks; San Juan Bautista's jail; the stables used by the hotel; a sheepherder's cabin moved into the park from its original site in the hills to the southeast; and the Castro and Zanetta Houses. Not included in the park but open to visitors daily from 9:30 to 5 is Mission San Juan Bautista, founded by Father Lasuen in 1797.

Castro House (below)

Castro House
1840–41

This two-story adobe with a red tile roof and full-length balcony was built by Gen. Jose Castro shortly after his appointment as prefect of Northern California. Castro intended the adobe to serve as his district's judicial and administrative headquarters. The house was little used by the flamboyant Mexican leader, however; his political and military activities called for extensive travel. In 1848 Castro deeded the adobe to San Juan's first English-speaking settlers, Patrick and Margaret Breen, who with their seven children had survived the tragic winter at Donner Lake in 1846–47. Successive generations of the Breen family occupied the house until it became part of San Juan Bautista State Historic Park in 1933. The interior has been refurnished in the style of the 1870s.

Zanetta House
1868

The two-story adobe-and-frame Zanetta House was constructed by Angelo Zanetta (proprietor of the Plaza Hotel, which still stands next to Castro House). The site had been occupied previously by a dormitory for unmarried mission Indian women, which later had been used by Gen. Jose Castro to quarter cavalrymen. Zanetta hoped that his building would be chosen as the courthouse of the newly established San Benito County. When Hollister was selected over San Juan Bautista, Zanetta modified the building's ground floor to serve as his home and turned the second floor into a public hall that became famous for the spring of its dance floor. Today Zanetta House is furnished with period antiques.

San Juan Bautista State Historic Park, San Juan Bautista, CA 95045; (408) 623-4881
Hours: 9–4:30 daily
Admission fee

(Courtesy of the California Department of Parks and Recreation)

San Luis Obispo

Dallidet Adobe
1853

A long arbor leads to this charming single-story adobe, which was built by the pioneer French vintner Paul Hyppolite Dallidet and occupied by his descendants for exactly a century. Deeded to the San Luis Obispo County Historical Society by Paul Dallidet in 1953, the house is now furnished in an eclectic manner with possessions of at least two generations of the family as well as items provided by the society. The garden is shaded by redwood trees; it features California native plants, and also a collection of horse-drawn vehicles. The carriage house was built with materials taken from Dallidet's original winery.

Dallidet Adobe, Pacific and Toro streets, San Luis Obispo, CA 93401
Hours: June through September, 1:30–4:30 each Sunday
Admission by donation

(Courtesy of the San Luis Obispo County Historical Society)

San Luis Obispo

Jack Residence
1878–80

Attractively framed by an old-fashioned garden, this two-story house with Italianate bracketing and a widow's walk was built between 1878 and 1880 for Robert E. Jack, a prosperous banker and land developer. It retains the Jack family's original furnishings, including the bedroom furniture of early-day movie actress Clara Kimball Young, which Mrs. Jack inadvertently purchased at a San Francisco auction by putting her hand to her face.

The home's dining room table, chairs and sideboard are Eastlake. Mrs. Jack's collection of Californiana is in the library, which has two thousand volumes.

Jack Residence, 536 Marsh Street, San Luis Obispo, CA 93406

Hours: The house is presently open to the public during community celebrations and by special arrangement with the Jack House Committee. Dates may be determined by inquiring of the San Luis Obispo Chamber of Commerce, 1039 Chorro, San Luis Obispo, CA 93406; (805) 543-1323.

(Courtesy of the City of San Luis Obispo Jack House Committee)

San Simeon

San Simeon State Historic Park (Hearst Castle) 1919–48

"The way God would have done it if he had had the money," was George Bernard Shaw's verdict after a visit to La Cuesta Encantada—"The Enchanted Hill." Between 1919 and 1948 William Randolph Hearst, head of an immense publishing, ranching and mining empire, and his architect Julia Morgan transformed a coastal knoll overlooking the Pacific into a legendary 123-acre estate of gardens, terraces and guest houses dominated by Hearst's residence, La Casa Grande.

The first structures to rise were three guest houses in the Mediterranean Renaissance style, La Casa del Mar, La Casa del Monte and La Casa del Sol, named according to their views. In 1922 work was begun on the great house, La Casa Grande, a Hispano Moresque structure of poured concrete faced with Utah limestone, with twin towers and copper domes housing bronze carillons from Belgium; its 100 rooms display Hearst's art treasures, furniture and antiques. Most impressive, perhaps, are both the assembly room and the refectory with its four-hundred-year-old hand-carved wooden ceiling brought from an Italian monastery and its musician's gallery.

The grounds are no less splendid. The outdoor Neptune swimming pool is constructed entirely of marble, surrounded by marble sculpture and set against the facade of a Greco-Roman temple. Formal gardens with tall cypresses and palms are complemented by compounds where imported wildlife roams freely; animals can be observed on the five-mile ride up from the castle entrance.

Hearst Castle is so large that, to see it all, one must take three separate two-hour tours. Tour 1 allows an overall impression, showing the gardens, the Neptune and Roman pools, a guest house and the main floor of La Casa Grande, including the refectory, assembly hall and movie theatre. Tour 2 visits La Casa Grande's upper floors, Hearst's private suite, the Celestial Suite, the libraries and the lobbies, as well as the gardens and pools. Also included are a duplex lodging and the kitchen. Tour 3 covers a guest wing, one guest house and the pools and gardens; it features works of art and furnishings. Comfortable walking shoes are strategic equipment here.

San Simeon State Historic Park, *San Simeon, CA 93452; (805) 927-4621 (for general information only; for reservations, see below)*

Hours: Tours are conducted daily except Thanksgiving, Christmas and New Year's days. Tours (of approximately 1¾ hours duration) begin at least every hour, during at least the period 8:20–3:20. The number of tours led is increased and the hours of operation are expanded during the summer. Ticket office open 8–4.

Admission fee

Reservations: Strongly advised. Reservations cannot be made by telephone. Tickets may be purchased in person from Ticketron agencies throughout California or at the Castle Visitor Center Ticket Office up to eight weeks in advance. (Group reservations can be made up to twelve weeks in advance.) Reservations can be made by mail by writing to San Simeon or to Ticketron, P.O. Box 26430, San Francisco, CA 94126; allow at least four weeks for processing and delivery. Envelopes should be marked "Hearst" and the date requested. Note that tickets cannot be left for pick up at Hearst Castle or at a temporary address, such as a hotel, and that Ticketron charges nominal reservation and cancellation service fees for each ticket.

(Courtesy of the California Department of Parks and Recreation)

The
Southland

Santa Barbara & Ventura Counties

Goleta

Stow House and Museum 1873

Originally a small, single-story structure built by Sherman P. Stow in 1873, this gracious ranch house with Gothic Revival features is one of the oldest landmarks in the Goleta Valley. During the ninety-five years it was owned by the Stows, Stow House served as the family home and the headquarters of their citrus farm, believed to be the site of the first commercial lemon plantings in California. It is now the headquarters of the Goleta Valley Historical Society.

Several of the ranch outbuildings still stand. The warehouse built by Sherman Stow in 1880 has been restored and converted into the Horace A. Sexton Memorial Museum. The blacksmith shop, formerly the garage, contains the tools and equipment of Goleta Valley's professional smith and historian, Jim Smith. The bunkhouse will house a library of documents important to the valley's history.

Stow House and Museum, 304 Los Carneros Road, Goleta, CA 93017; (805) 964-4407 Hours: 2–4 Saturday and Sunday; closed during January

(Courtesy of the Goleta Valley Historical Society)

Stow House (opposite)

Santa Barbara

Fernald House
1860; altered 1880

In 1851 Charles Fernald set out for Maine and home after trying his luck in the California goldfields. He had also gained some knowledge of the law in San Francisco; and before taking leave of the state he paused in Santa Barbara, where he was persuaded to remain as sheriff. Nine years later, still in Santa Barbara and now a county court judge, Fernald commissioned a local cabinet maker, Rosewell Forbush, to build a simple, two-story brick house with a pitched roof. Although almost completely altered to Queen Anne style in 1880 by the architects Thomas Nixon and Peter J. Barber, Fernald House still has Forbush's handsome woodwork. The curved mahogany staircase is particularly fine.

After the death in 1958 of the last of Judge Fernald's children, the house was donated to the Santa Barbara Historical Society and moved to its present site. Many of the Fernald family's original furnishings, including paintings, books and personal belongings, may be seen.

Fernald House, 414 West Montecito Street, Santa Barbara, CA 93101; (805) 966-1601
Hours: 2–4 Sunday
Admission fee

(Courtesy of the Santa Barbara Historical Society)

Santa Barbara

Trussell-Winchester Adobe
1854

A Maine Yankee, Capt. Horatio Gates Trussell, built this charming adobe for his bride, Ramona Burke, great-granddaughter of one of the mutineers of the *Bounty*. Considered an excellent example of the transitional period when American wood frame construction was superseding the Spanish adobe style, the house combines a central section of sun-dried adobe bricks with a high-pitched gable roof and frame wings characteristic of New England. Timbers and brass salvaged from the *Winfield Scott*, wrecked off Anacapa Island in 1853, were incorporated in the house.

The Trussell family made the adobe their home for fifteen years; thereafter it had several owners, and in 1953 the house, its furnishings and grounds were bequeathed the Santa Barbara Historical Society. Some of the collection of period furnishings and paintings are original to the house.

Trussell-Winchester Adobe, 412 West Montecito Street, Santa Barbara, CA 93101; (805) 966-1601
Hours: 2–4 Sunday

(Courtesy of the Santa Barbara Historical Society)

Simi Valley

R.P. Strathearn Historical Park

Simi Valley's historical park includes two pre-twentieth-century structures, one of which was built around a now-rare eighteenth-century home, an adobe. Also in the park are the Simi library and a collection of early farming implements, and soon the St. Rose of Lima Catholic Church (1898) will be relocated here.

Strathearn House
1893

When cattle rancher R. P. Strathearn incorporated an old two-room adobe in his frame Victorian home, he incidentally preserved one of the few remaining structures erected in California before 1800. The original Simi Adobe, probably little more than a mud hut, had been built by Santiago Pico and Luis Peña to secure their rights to 100,000-acre Rancho Simi, in 1795; Strathearn converted the adobe to use as his dining room and kitchen.

The house was occupied, with little alteration, by members of the family from the 1890s until 1968. The front garden is much the way the first Mrs. Strathearn knew it.

Colony House
1888

The cottage near Strathearn House recalls the razzle-dazzle promotions of Southern California's pioneer real estate dealers during the 1880s. Enticed by advertisements showing steamboats on a river that in fact exists only briefly after a cloudburst, and by the promise of a salubrious climate, a group of Eastern doctors purchased lots from the Simi Land and Water Company to establish a health resort. Colony House is one of twelve prefabricated cottages shipped here by rail to give substance to their dream. But when Simiopolis, as they called it, proved to be only a paper town on the banks of a dry arroyo, and in a desert valley at the foot of desolate mountains, the doctors lost heart and returned home. The little houses remained to become the nucleus of modern Simi. Only two exist today. Colony House was brought to its present site in the 1970s and is furnished with a miscellany of belongings donated by descendants of Simi Valley's early families.

R.P. Strathearn Historical Park, 137 Strathearn Place, Simi Valley, CA 93065; (805) 526-6453
Hours: 1–4 Sunday; closed Christmas, New Year's, Easter and Mother's days and during wet weather

(Courtesy of the Simi Valley Historical Society)

Colony House (above)

San Fernando Valley

Calabasas

The Leonis Adobe
ca. 1844; enlarged 1870s

In a time when colorful figures were commonplace, Miguel Leonis stood head and shoulders above the crowd. The giant Basque, reputedly so daring and accomplished a smuggler in his native French Pyrenees that he had found it wiser to seek his fortune overseas, arrived in Los Angeles some time in the mid-1800s. Speaking little English or Spanish hampered him not a whit in carving out a sizeable empire in land and livestock in the western San Fernando Valley; Leonis protected his interests vigorously with an armed retinue of Indians and Mexicans, and he developed a fine talent for influencing decisions in the Los Angeles courts. His marriage to a wealthy Indian widow, Espiritu Chujilla, greatly increased his holdings.

The home and ranch headquarters of "The King of Calabasas" was originally a simple two-story adobe put up in the 1840s. Leonis remodeled and enlarged the building in the Monterey Colonial style during the 1870s, adding the Victorian fretwork balcony and wooden flooring. His home has been restored to the way it probably appeared after the remodeling, and it is furnished appropriately for the period. The Leonis family portraits hang in the living room in their original places.

The Leonis Adobe, 23537 Calabasas Road, Calabasas, CA 91302; (213) 346-3683
Hours: 1–4 Wednesday, Saturday and Sunday and also Memorial Day, the Fourth of July and Labor Day

(Courtesy of the Leonis Adobe Association)

Encino

Los Encinos State Historic Park

Los Encinos State Historic Park preserves five acres of the 4,460-acre Rancho El Encino granted to Vincente de la Ossa in 1845, but the history of the rancho lands is rooted in the eighteenth century and Spain's efforts to extend its control up the Pacific coast. It was here, on a blistering August afternoon in 1769, that Gaspar de Portola and his party of explorers came upon a large body of water, warm springs and broad grazing lands near what is now the town of Encino. "It was a pleasant place to stop," Father Crespi noted in his diary. Today, with old buildings, an orange grove, vineyard and plants of the mission and rancho periods clustered about a lake, Los Encinos remains a pleasant place to visit.

De la Ossa Adobe
1849

Don Vicente de la Ossa, who acquired Rancho El Encino in 1845, built this single-story adobe with porticos running the length of each side. Architecturally unchanged, it has been restored and furnished to illustrate life on the ranch throughout its two-hundred-year history, using photographs and period accessories and furniture that belonged to former owners.

Garnier Building
1872

After de la Ossa's death the ranch was purchased by Philippe and Eugene Garnier, sheep farmers from the French Basque country. They dug the guitar-shaped lake, walled up the spring, and built this two-story French Provincial house modeled on their family home. Constructed of rough stone laid up in mortar, it was then plastered with cement and lined out to resemble stone. An exterior staircase at the rear of the building provided access to the upper story.

Los Encinos State Historic Park, 16756 *Moorpark Street, Encino, CA 91316; (213) 784-4849*
Hours: House; 1–4 Wednesday–Sunday; grounds; 8–5 daily

(Courtesy of the California Department of Parks and Recreation and the Encino Historical Society, Inc.)

Mentryville

Mentry House
ca. 1880

California's first commercially successful oil well was drilled in Pico Canyon by Charles Alexander Mentry in 1876. All that remains of the pioneer oil town of Mentryville, which sprang up nearby, are the schoolhouse, a barn and the thirteen-room home Mentry built for his family in the early 1880s. The house has been restored and furnished with period antiques by the Lagasse family and is shown by appointment only.

Mentry House, 27201 West Pico Canyon Road, Mentryville, CA 91321
Hours: By appointment only; write to Mrs. Carol Lagasse at Mentry House

(*Courtesy of the Newhall Woman's Club and the Santa Clarita Valley Historical Society*)

Mission Hills

Andres Pico Adobe
ca. 1834

Not far from the Mission San Fernando Rey is the second-oldest house in Los Angeles, a two-story adobe dating in part from about 1834. In 1846 it passed with the purchase of the vast mission lands to Eulegio de Celis; on his death in 1853 it formed part of the half-interest in the rancho purchased by General Andres Pico, brother of Mexican California's last governor. Pico preferred the mission *convento* as his home and turned over the little adobe to his adopted son, Romulo, who added a second story in 1873. By 1930, when the curator of the Southwest Museum decided to purchase and restore it, little was left but the walls and legends of ghostly occupants. Now headquarters of the San Fernando Historical Society, the adobe is furnished with antiques of the period in which the Picos lived.

Andres Pico Adobe, 10940 Sepulveda Boulevard, Mission Hills, CA 91340; (213) 365-7810
Hours: 1–4 Wednesday–Sunday

(*Courtesy of the San Fernando Valley Historical Society, Inc.*)

Newhall

William S. Hart Park and Museum
1925–28

In 1921 cowboy movie star William S. Hart purchased the old Horseshoe Ranch in the Santa Clarita Valley at the foot of the San Gabriel Mountains. Here, with the help of his sister, he designed and built "La Loma de Los Vientos" (The Hill of the Winds), considered an outstanding example of Spanish-Mexican architecture. In appreciation for the nickels, dimes and quarters the public had paid to see his movies, Hart bequeathed the ranch, house and its contents to the city of Newhall. On display are the original furnishings, historical weapons and mementos of the American theater as well as Hart's collection of Western art, which includes works by Charles M. Russell and Frederic Remington.

Near the park entrance is the original ranch house, a batten-and-board structure built in 1910. Often used as a movie set, it houses early motion-picture props and a collection of hand-tooled saddles. The walls of the bunkhouse nearby are decorated with watercolor sketches of "Cowboy Bill" by John Norval Marchand.

William S. Hart Park and Museum, 24151 *Newhall Avenue, Newhall, CA 91321; (805) 259-0855*

Hours: Museum, 10–3 Wednesday–Friday and 10–5 Saturday–Sunday, closed holidays; park, open daily 10–5 during standard time and 10–7:30 daylight saving time, closed holidays

(Courtesy of the City of Los Angeles Park and Recreation Department and the William S. Hart Park and Museum)

San Fernando

La Casa de Geronimo Lopez
1882–83

San Fernando's oldest adobe is a singularly attractive two-story residence, regarded as an outstanding example of California's transitional architecture combining the early Spanish and American styles. The house was built by Valentin Lopez, son of the *mayordomo* (manager) of Mission San Fernando who occupied the casa for about a year before its acquisition by his sister and brother-in-law, Catalina and Geronimo Lopez. During their lives the casa was a center of San Fernando life; the Lopezes played a significant role in the history of San Fernando Valley. They opened the first school teaching in English, started the first post office and the first general store, and operated the Butterfield stage house on their Lopez Station ranch. Today, repainted the original white and turquoise and restored to its original floor plan, the house appears much as the Lopezes knew it. Furnishings are from the period 1853–1910.

La Casa de Geronimo Lopez, 1100 *Pico Street, San Fernando, CA 91340*
Hours: 11–3 Wednesday and Saturday, 1–4 Sunday; closed December 24–January 2
Admission fee

(*Courtesy of the Lopez Adobe Historical Site and Preservation Commission*)

Central L.A. & the Beach

Compton

Dominguez Ranch Adobe
1826

The history of the Dominguez Ranch Adobe may be said to begin in 1769, when Juan Jose Dominguez, a veteran soldier, guide and interpreter, marched up from Mexico with Gaspar de Portola and Father Serra to take possession of California for Spain. In 1782 he was rewarded for his services to the Spanish crown with a land grant of more than 75,000 acres— the first such concession in California— embracing all the harbor area south of the Pueblo de Los Angeles. Juan Jose's grand-nephew, Manuel, inherited the ranch, and he built a six-room adobe on it in 1826. Over the years the house has undergone substantial alterations and additions and is now part of the Claretian Order's Dominguez Seminary. Several rooms, including Don Manuel's original six, have been restored as a historical museum, displaying furnishings and memorabilia of the Dominguez family.

Dominguez Ranch Adobe, *18127 South Alameda Street, Compton, CA 90220; (213) 631-5981 or 636-6030*
Hours: 1–4 Tuesday, Wednesday and the second and third Sundays of each month

(Courtesy of the Claretian Fathers of Dominguez Seminary)

Inglewood

La Casa de la Centinela Adobe 1834

This charming little adobe, considered one of the best preserved in the Los Angeles area, was formerly the main house of Rancho Aguaje del Centinela, granted to Ignacio Machado in 1844. It was built at least ten years earlier; old records speak of a three-room house with a flat brea (tar) roof and walls of sun-dried bricks. Restored, reroofed with shake shingles and furnished with nineteenth-century antiques, it is now the headquarters of the Historical Society of Centinela Valley. Two olive trees planted more than 140 years ago still stand in the gardens.

La Casa de la Centinela Adobe, 7634 Midfield Avenue, Inglewood, CA 90045; (213) 649-7483
Hours: 2–4 Wednesday and Sunday
Admission by donation
(Courtesy of the Historical Society of Centinela Valley)

La Casa de la Centinela Adobe (below)

Long Beach

Rancho Los Alamitos
1806; enlarged in the 1840s and 1900–1925

One of the oldest houses in California is the ranch house at Rancho Los Alamitos, whose main, adobe portion dates from 1806. Juan Jose Neito built it, on land awarded to his father by Governor Pedro Fages in 1784. In 1842 the ranch and house were acquired by the wealthy Yankee merchant-landowner Don Abel Stearns, who added the wooden north wing as a bunkhouse. The south wing and second story, dating from the early years of this century, were built by the Bixby ranching family, which purchased Los Alamitos in 1881.

By 1968 the ranch had dwindled from its original 28,500 acres to approximately 7½; that year it was donated by the Bixbys to the city of Long Beach as an historic site. The charming old ranch house is shown with furnishings that belonged to the Bixbys, and its outbuildings are surrounded by 5 acres of formal gardens that include the garden started by Stearns in the 1850s.

Rancho Los Alamitos, 6400 *East Bixby Hill Road, Long Beach, CA* 90815; (213) 431-2511
Hours: 1–5 Wednesday-Friday; closed holidays; guided tours only

(Courtesy of the City of Long Beach Public Library)

Long Beach

Rancho Los Cerritos
1844; enlarged thereafter

In 1843 Jonathan (Don Juan) Temple, one of the first Americans to settle in California, purchased 27,000 acres of the 1784 Los Nietos land grant, and a year later he began building this large, two-story adobe ranch house. Temple combined the traditional Spanish-Mexican U-shaped plan with the double galleried structure developed by Thomas Larkin at his home in Monterey. Between 1866 and 1954 the Bixby ranching family lived here, enlarging the house, and substituting a pitched roof in the New England style. Today this romantic monument to Mexican California is a museum and research library, furnished with antiques and exhibits intended to portray the history and life of the ranch. Some of the original trees and shrubs planted in Don Juan Temple's time remain in the garden.

Rancho Los Cerritos, 6400 *Virginia Road, Long Beach, CA* 90807; (213) 424-9423
Hours: 1–5 Wednesday-Sunday; closed Thanksgiving, Christmas and New Year's days

(Courtesy of the City of Long Beach Public Library)

Los Angeles

Avila Adobe
1818
El Pueblo de Los Angeles State Historic Park

The narrow passageway leading from Olvera Street to the courtyard of Los Angeles' oldest dwelling serves as a time corridor bridging more than 160 years. Here, while the Plaza Church was still being constructed and the city numbered fewer than six hundred souls, the prosperous cattle rancher Don Francisco Avila constructed an adobe townhouse with 2½-foot-thick walls, high ceiling, a covered porch, a chapel and, most impressive at the time, the first French doors in the pueblo. The adobe was in the possession of the Avila and Rimpau families for 110 years. An earthquake brought down more than half of the building in 1870, and today only a wing remains of the original eighteen-room structure. This is now a part of El Pueblo de Los Angeles State Historic Park, restored and refurnished to appear as it might have in the 1840s.

Avila Adobe, 14 Olvera Street, Los Angeles, CA 90012; (213) 628-1274
Hours: 10–3 Tuesday-Friday; 10–4:30 Saturday and Sunday
Admission fee

(Courtesy of the California Department of Parks and Recreation)

Los Angeles

Casa de Adobe
1916

The atmosphere of early California's great ranchos has been preserved in this exact and attractive replica of a prosperous Spanish Colonial hacienda built about 1800. Constructed with meticulous attention to the methods and materials used by the first Spanish settlers, the Casa de Adobe follows the plan of the earliest type, with single-story rooms entirely enclosing a patio for protection. In typical style the casa includes not only a formal entrance, sitting rooms, bedrooms and a separate dining room and kitchen but a bathroom, dispensary, chapel, and quarters for the priest and ranch hands. As the Casa de Adobe is intended to portray the home life of a California family over a period of fifty years, furnishings from several periods and such equipment as branding irons, lariats, even muskets and swords fill the rooms. The patio garden has been planted with shrubs and flowering plants that the first Spanish settlers would have known.

Casa de Adobe, 4605 North Figueroa Street, Los Angeles, CA 90042; (213) 225-8653
Hours: 1–4:45 Wednesday, Saturday and Sunday

(Courtesy of the Southwest Museum)
Casa de Adobe (above)

Los Angeles

El Alisal
1897–1910

El Alisal (the sycamore) is a remarkable house built by a remarkable man. Charles Fletcher Lummis, editor, author, explorer, founder of the Southwest Museum and Los Angeles city librarian, constructed his stone castle virtually singlehandedly over a period of fourteen years. Using granite boulders found on the property, concrete, telephone poles scrounged from the Santa Fe Railroad and hardware gathered on his travels in Mexico and Peru, Lummis built, he said, "to last a thousand years." He achieved a unique home that hints of the Southwest and of medieval Europe. In this romantic setting Lummis entertained the leading intellectuals and artists of the day, among them John Muir, Carrie Jacobs Bond, Helena Modjeska and Carl Sandburg. When Lummis died in 1928, his ashes were sealed within the patio wall.

El Alisal is now headquarters of the Historical Society of Southern California. The rooms that are shown contain a few of the original furnishings, photographs of Lummis's family, his books and personal mementos.

El Alisal, 200 East Avenue 43, Los Angeles, CA 90031; (213) 222-0546
Hours: 1–4 Wednesday-Sunday

(Courtesy of the Historical Society of Southern California)

Los Angeles

Ennis-Brown House
1924

The Ennis-Brown House is, like Frank Lloyd Wright's earlier-built Hollyhock House in Barnsdall Park, a powerful example of the influence of Mayan temple architecture on Wright's work in the early 1920s. The house is magnificently situated on a hillside overlooking Los Angeles. Its walls incline with a pyramid effect; the ornamentation is geometric; and a cavelike entrance hall enhances the dramatic impact of the interior's varied ceiling heights and contrasting illumination. No expense was spared on this house. There is a 100-foot-long marble gallery, and the living room has a fireplace that is the remaining example of only four glass mosaics Wright ever designed. The numerous stained-glass windows were executed by Orlando Giannini to Wright's designs. Teakwood was used for all the walls and ceilings.

Built for Charles F. Ennis and his wife, the house is still a private residence; it is occupied by G. Oliver Brown, who has donated it to the Trust for Preservation of Cultural Heritage. Public tours are conducted on six days of the year only, and reservations are required.

Ennis-Brown House, 2607 *Glendower Avenue, Los Angeles, CA 90027; (213) 660-0051*

Hours: Tours conducted on the second Sunday of every odd month by reservation only; requests for reservations should be made in writing to the Trust for Preservation of Cultural Heritage, 2655 Glendower Avenue, Los Angeles, CA 90027

Admission fee

(Courtesy of the Trust for Preservation of Cultural Heritage)

Los Angeles

Heritage Square

In Heritage Square, just off the Pasadena Freeway at Avenue 43, the Cultural Heritage Foundation has created a sanctuary for historic Los Angeles buildings threatened by the wrecker's ball. In time the square will replicate a Victorian village, preserving for the future some fifteen houses, a church, a schoolhouse, a railroad depot and other significant structures of the period 1860–1910. Already located there are Hale House (1888), with elements of Queen Anne and Eastlake styles; Mount Pleasant (1876), an Italianate house; Beaudry House (1887), which is Queen Anne and Italianate; the Valley Knudsen Garden Residence (1877), in French Mansard style; the Victorian Gothic Palms Railroad Station (1885); the Lincoln Avenue Methodist Church (1897), which is Carpenter Gothic and Queen Anne; and a carriage house. Currently only Hale House may be toured; the other buildings are seen from the outside only.

Hale House
1888

Combining the Eastlake and Queen Anne styles, Hale House is an exuberant example of Los Angeles residential architecture in the 1880s. It was constructed almost entirely of California redwood and boasts fish-scale shingles, ornate brick chimneys, exterior wood carving and a Queen Anne turret surmounted by a large copper fleur-de-lis. Furnishings, while not original to the house, are representative of the period.

Very little is known about the history of Hale House, which stood at the corner of Avenue Forty-Five and Figueroa in the Mount Washington district before its removal to Heritage Square in 1970. Neither the architect nor its first owners have been identified. In 1901 it was purchased by James and Bessie Hale; after Mr. Hale's death, Mrs. Hale converted their home into a boarding house, living there until her death in 1967.

Heritage Square, 3800 *Homer Street, Los Angeles,* CA 90031; (213) 222-3150
Hours: 11–3 *the first and second Sundays and the third Wednesday of each month*
Admission fee

(Courtesy of the City of Los Angeles Cultural Heritage Board)

Los Angeles

Hollyhock House
1919–21

"A very proud house," is the way Frank Lloyd Wright described Hollyhock House, the first of the residences he designed in Los Angeles. Intended as the principal structure of a center for the arts commissioned by oil heiress Aline Barnsdall, the house resembles a Mayan temple poised on an acropolis, with each room overlooking a garden or a reflecting pool. Ms. Barnsdall deeded her home and its outbuildings to the city of Los Angeles in 1927. Restored and refurbished in 1975, it is now used for official functions and retains a few of Wright's original furnishings.

Hollyhock House, Barnsdall Park, 4808 Hollywood Boulevard, Los Angeles, CA 90027; (213) 662-7272
Hours: By tour only; at 10, 11, 12 and 1 on Tuesday and Thursday, and at 12, 1, 2 and 3 on Saturday and the first and third Sundays of each month
Admission fee

(Courtesy of the City of Los Angeles Cultural Heritage Board)

Los Angeles

R. M. Schindler House
1921–22

Hidden by a lush tangle of hedges and trees on West Hollywood's Kings Road is a benchmark in the development of California residential architecture. Rudolph Schindler, the Austrian-born architect who came to Los Angeles with Frank Lloyd Wright in 1920, designed and built this house as a cooperative dwelling for his own family and their friends, the Clyde Chases. It served as a proving ground for innovations of Schindler's—sliding doors, glass walls, the use of landscaping as an architectural element, tilt-slab construction—that have become widely accepted elements of the California home. The house was acquired by the Friends of the Schindler House in 1977 and now serves as a center for the study of architecture in Los Angeles.

R. M. Schindler House, 833 North Kings Road, Los Angeles, CA 90069; (213) 651-1510
Hours: 11–4 Saturday, and by appointment
Admission fee

(Courtesy of the Friends of the Schindler House)

Pacific Palisades

Will Rogers State Historic Park
1928

Originally a small weekend cottage, cowboy philosopher Will Rogers' ranch home is a comfortable, rambling two-story structure in a rustic indeterminate style. Will resided here from 1928 until his death in a plane crash in 1935, continually enlarging the home to its present thirty-one rooms. It contains much personal memorabilia of the famous humorist, including a stuffed calf given him by friends as a more appropriate object of his roping skills than themselves. The 186-acre grounds are laced with trails laid out by Rogers; his polo field is still used for the game he loved so well.

Will Rogers State Historic Park, 14253 *Sunset Boulevard, Pacific Palisades, CA 90272; (213) 454-8212*
Hours: House, 10–5 daily; grounds, 8–5 daily; closed Thanksgiving, Christmas and New Year's days
Admission fee

(Courtesy of the California Department of Parks and Recreation)

Santa Monica

Heritage Square Museum
(Roy Jones House)
1894

Originally the home of Roy Jones, son of Santa Monica's founder, this American Colonial Revival house was designed by Sumner P. Hunt, the architect of the Southwest Museum. In 1981 Roy Jones House, too, was opened as a community museum, with period rooms, changing exhibits pertaining to Santa Monica's history and culture, a museum shop, and a library. Some of the original furniture has been located and restored to the house.

Heritage Square Museum (Roy Jones House), *2612 Main Street, Santa Monica, CA 90405; (213) 392-8537*
Hours: 11–4 Thursday-Saturday

(Courtesy of the Santa Monica Heritage Square Museum Society)

Roy Jones House (above)

Wilmington

Drum Barracks Civil War Museum
1862

All that remains of the Union Army's headquarters for Southern California and Arizona is this handsomely proportioned frame building surrounded by tall palms and cypress trees. Built in the Colonial style, the officers' quarters of Drum Barracks, though later converted to a private residence, retains its original sixteen rooms, fireplaces and porches. The original paint and cypress shingle roof are still in good condition. The barracks now serve as a museum of the Civil War period, but among the military artifacts and furnishings are items of a more domestic nature, such as the chandelier from which each occupant would take a lighted candle to find his way to bed.

Drum Barracks' history was short but significant. Although far removed from the main arenas of the Civil War, partisan feeling ran high on the Pacific Coast; to ensure its loyalty, the Union leaders established military posts throughout the West. From 1862 until its disbandment in 1866, the Drum Barracks garrison, with its supply depot and a station for the colorful but ineffective camel corps, dampened the enthusiasms of Los Angeles secessionists.

Drum Barracks Civil War Museum, 1053 *Cary Avenue, Wilmington, CA 90744; (213) 518-1955 (5–8)*
Hours: 1–4 on the first and last full weekends each month
Admission by donation

(Courtesy of the Society for the Preservation of Drum Barracks)

Wilmington

Gen. Phineas Banning Residence Museum
1864

Redolent of the romantic Old South, the lovely Greek Revival mansion that Phineas Banning designed for himself stands in a large park a little to the north of the point where he altered the course of Los Angeles's history by developing a deep-water shipping channel in San Pedro Bay. Banning, grandson of a founder of the state of Delaware, arrived in California in 1851. Bluff and energetic, with a keen appreciation of the importance of transportation, he pioneered freight and passenger lines, founded the town of Wilmington, negotiated key rail links and constructed the harbor breakwaters, assuring the phenomenal growth of Southern California.

Throughout Banning's lifetime, his house was the center of a glittering social life, and it was a rallying place for supporters of the Union and abolitionist causes. It remained in the Banning family until 1925 and was purchased by the city of Los Angeles two years later.

The home's construction is of California redwood, fashioned by ship's carpenters whose captains exchanged their services for tar from the La Brea pits, twenty miles north. The handsomely proportioned rooms are furnished with period antiques that number among them forty-two pieces contributed by Phineas Banning's descendants.

Gen. Phineas Banning Residence Museum, 401 *East M Street, Wilmington, CA 90744; (213) 548-7777*
Hours: 1–4 Wednesday, Saturday and Sunday

(Courtesy of the Gen. Phineas Banning Residence Museum)

Pasadena & Bordering Towns

Arcadia

Hugo Reid Adobe
1840

Soon after receiving provisional title to the 13,319-acre Rancho Santa Anita, Don Perfecto (Hugo) Reid, Scottish-born adventurer and naturalized Mexican citizen, and his Indian wife, Victoria, erected a modest ranch house as proof of their intent to settle. "Flat roof'd and corridor'd," it was built of sun-dried adobe bricks, roofed with cane that had been waterproofed with tar from the La Brea pits, and whitewashed with lime. This reconstruction of Reid's adobe contains handmade furnishings characteristic of the California period as well as memorabilia of his travels in the Pacific.

Hugo Reid Adobe, *Los Angeles State and County Arboretum, 301 North Baldwin Avenue, Arcadia, CA 91006; (213) 446-8251*
Hours: 9–4:30 daily
Admission fee

(Courtesy of the Los Angeles State and County Arboretum)

Arcadia

Queen Anne Cottage
1885–86

Lucky in money but not in love, millionaire speculator Elias Jackson ("Lucky") Baldwin began building this charming cottage for his fourth wife, who left him before it was completed. It became instead a memorial to his third, the lovely Jennie Dexter. Although termed "Queen Anne," the cottage is actually a combination of the Queen Anne, Stick and Eastlake styles. On Baldwin's death in 1909 it was closed and its furnishings dispersed, and it stood neglected until restored in 1951–53. The cottage has been furnished with appropriate Victoriana, including portraits of Baldwin and Jennie Dexter. Nearby is the opulent carriage house, in which Baldwin housed as many as fourteen vehicles as well as his carriage horses.

Queen Anne Cottage, *Los Angeles State and County Arboretum, 301 North Baldwin Avenue, Arcadia, CA 91006; (213) 446-8251
Hours: 9–4:30 daily
Admission fee*

(Courtesy of the Los Angeles State and County Arboretum)

Glendale

Brand Library and Art Center
(El Miradero)
1902-4

High in the foothills overlooking Glendale and the San Fernando Valley is one of Southern California's most striking residences. "El Miradero," designed in the Saracenic style for Leslie C. Brand, was inspired by the East Indian Pavilion at the 1893 Chicago World's Fair. In accordance with Mr. Brand's bequest to the city of Glendale, it is today a public art and music library; the grounds are a public park.

Brand Library and Art Center, 1601 West Mountain Street, Glendale, CA 91201; (213) 956-2051

Hours: 12–9 Tuesday and Thursday, 12–6 Wednesday, Friday and Saturday; docent tours by appointment

(Courtesy of the Brand Library and Art Center)

Glendale

Casa Adobe de San Rafael
1867–71

On retiring as Los Angeles's first sheriff, Tomas Sanchez built this single-story adobe with fifteen-inch-thick walls on a portion of the vast Jose Maria Verdugo rancho granted him by the Verdugos. Surrounded by wide verandas on three sides, the building retains its original floors and ceilings, and it is furnished with late-nineteenth-century antiques that include a painted mirror once owned by California's last Mexican governor, Pio Pico.

Casa Adobe de San Rafael, 1330 Dorothy
  Drive, Glendale, CA 91214
Hours: June 24–September 1, 1–4 Wednesday
  and Sunday

(Courtesy of the City of Glendale Parks and Recreation
Division and Glendale Beautiful)

Monrovia

George H. Anderson House
1886

Typical of the modest houses that mushroomed throughout the Los Angeles area during the real estate boom of the 1880s, this Carpenter Gothic cottage is one of Monrovia's earliest buildings. It was erected by John C. Anderson, an Ohio-born contractor who worked on the town's first hotel, and was continually occupied by the Anderson family until 1974. Furnishings, though not original to the house, are characteristic of the turn of the century; among the most interesting pieces are an 1820 tilt-top table from Virginia and bird's-eye-maple bedroom furniture.

George H. Anderson House, 215 East Lime
  Avenue, Monrovia, CA 91016
Hours: 12–4 the third Sunday of each month

(Courtesy of the Monrovia Historical Society)
Anderson House (above)

Pasadena

Gamble House
1908

This outstanding example of the American Craftsman–style bungalow houses designed by Charles and Henry Greene was built as a winter home for David B. Gamble, a member of the Procter and Gamble firm. Situated on a hill commanding magnificent views of the San Gabriels, it is somewhat Japanese in feeling, with overhanging eaves supported by heavy, hand-shaped beams, open sleeping porches and a shingled exterior stained a muted shade of olive. Hand- rubbed wood paneling and exquisite craftsmanship characterize the interiors. The furnishings, save for the Gustav Stickley furniture used in two of the bedrooms, were all designed by the Greenes. A dominant feature of the house is the three-panel Tiffany-glass front door with a gnarled-oak design executed in earth tones.

Gamble House, 4 *Westmoreland Place, Pasadena,* CA 91103; (213) 793-3334
Hours: 10–3 Tuesday, Thursday and the last Sunday of each month
Admission fee

(Courtesy of the Gamble House and the Greene and Greene Library)

Pasadena

Pasadena Historical Society Museum (Fenyes Mansion) 1905
Finnish Folk Exhibit

This spacious and formal mansion was designed by Robert Farquhar for Dr. Adelbert Fenyes, the son of a Hungarian aristocrat, and his American wife, Eva Scott Muse Fenyes. It contains a wealth of memorabilia, antiques and portraits accumulated over three generations by a family with a considerable interest in the arts. Mrs. Fenyes, herself a talented musician and artist, was succeeded in ownership by her daughter, Mrs. Thomas Curtin, author of several books on the Southwest. In 1946 Mrs. Curtin's daughter Leonora married Y. A Paloheimo, Finnish consul for the Southwest and founder of the Finlandia Foundation. The house then served as the Finnish Consulate, until 1970.

The Fenyes Mansion, made available with all its contents to the Pasadena Historical Society, is now the society's headquarters and museum. On the grounds is the Finnish Folk Exhibit, displaying folk art and antiques characteristic of Finnish farmhouses two centuries ago.

Pasadena Historical Society Museum, 470 *West Walnut Street, Pasadena, CA 91103; (213) 577-1660*
Hours: 1–4 Tuesdays and Thursdays, and on the last Sunday of each month; guided tours only
Admission by donation

(Courtesy of the Pasadena Historical Society)

Pasadena

Wrigley Mansion
1906–1914

Eight years in the planning and the building, this classic white mansion in the Italian Renaissance style is impressive even among the stately homes of Pasadena's "Millionaires Row." It was the joint endeavor of George W. Stimson, a successful real estate promoter, and his architect son Lawrence. Rare and costly woods, such as Circassian walnut and the extinct crotch mahogany from the Philippines, and the mansion's antique Chinese silver-foil wallpaper (ca. 1835) are notable features.

The mansion proved too large for the Stimsons' needs and was purchased by the chewing gum magnate William Wrigley, Jr., in 1914; on his widow's death in 1959 it was donated to the city of Pasadena as headquarters for the Tournament of Roses Association. (The Rosebowl Room houses a collection of memorabilia of all the Rosebowl games.) Palm trees planted by George Stimson and extensive rose gardens are particularly lovely features of the surrounding grounds.

Wrigley Mansion, *391 South Orange Grove Boulevard, Pasadena, CA 91105; (213) 449-4100 or 681-3724*
Hours: House, 2–4 February–September, Wednesday afternoons; guided tours at 2, 2:30, 3 and 3:30; gardens, open daily

(Courtesy of the Pasadena Tournament of Roses Association)

San Gabriel

La Casa Vieja de Lopez
1783–85; altered 1870 and
1920s

One of the oldest houses described in this book is La Casa Vieja de Lopez, originally one of a row of adobe buildings that formed the west wall of the Mission San Gabriel quadrangle. The casa's early history is uncertain. Until the secularization of the missions in 1832, it was probably used for storage, perhaps as a workroom; certainly it was in ruins when Nepomuceno Juan Lopez, a blacksmith from Sonora, Mexico, acquired the property in 1870. Lopez rebuilt what was left of the structure as a residence with a pitched roof of wooden shingles, small rooms and dirt floors, which he and his descendants continued to improve for nearly a century. Maria Guadaloupe Lopez de Lowther, the last of the family to occupy the house, added the attractive patio with an octagonal fountain.

Today the adobe is again the property of Mission San Gabriel, used to house archival materials and to display a collection of seventeenth- and eighteenth-century religious art from Mexico and Spain. Among the artifacts brought here from other early adobes in the area are three pieces of furniture that belonged to the Lopez family and portraits of Don Juan and Maria.

La Casa Vieja de Lopez, 330 South Anita Avenue, San Gabriel, CA 91776; (213) 282-5191
Hours: 1–4 Wednesday and Sunday and by appointment
Admission fee

(Courtesy of the Mission San Gabriel and Fordham W. R. Peterson)

San Marino

Huntington Library, Art Gallery and Botanical Gardens
1910; 1925

The former home of Henry E. Huntington, railroad magnate and philanthropist, now houses the art gallery of this renowned educational institution. Designed in 1910 by Myron Hunt and Elmer Grey, the former home itself is a two-story Italianate structure with a lengthy columned portico. British and French art of the eighteenth and nineteenth centuries dominate the collections; among the best-known works are Gainsborough's *Blue Boy*, Lawrence's *Pinkie* and Constable's *View on the Stour*. There is also a small, important collection of Renaissance bronze statues.

The adjacent library was built in 1925 to house Huntington's extraordinary collection of manuscripts, incunabula, English and American first editions, and more than half a million other books. A selection of some two hundred special treasures is always displayed, among them a Gutenberg Bible, the Ellesmere manuscript of Chaucer's *Canterbury Tales*, a first folio of Shakespeare's plays, and Benjamin Franklin's *Autobiography* in manuscript.

The buildings stand amidst gardens of unusual beauty. Linked by expansive lawns are a Shakespeare garden, growing plants mentioned by "Sweet Will"; a Japanese garden with a moon bridge arched above a pond; and extensive plantings of palms, roses and camellias. The twelve-acre desert garden contains the largest outdoor collection of desert plants in the world.

Huntington Library, Art Gallery and Botanical Gardens, 1151 Oxford Road, San Marino, CA 91108. From San Marino or Pasadena, call (213) 792-6141; from Los Angeles or elsewhere, (213) 681-6601. For Sunday ticket information, (213) 449-3901

Hours: 1–4:30 Tuesday-Sunday; closed Mondays, major holidays and October 1–31. Docent tours Tuesday-Friday. Sunday visitors must make reservations.

(Courtesy of the Huntington Library, Art Gallery and Botanical Gardens)

Huntington Library (opposite)

Neighboring Towns to the East

City of Industry

Workman and Temple Homestead

This site preserves three important landmarks in the history of Southern California, on a portion of the 1845 Rancho La Puente land grant.

Workman Home
1844; altered 1869

The core of this Victorian Gothic house is a simple adobe hacienda built by William Workman, who, with his business partner John Rowland, led the first group of American overland settlers to the San Gabriel Valley, in 1841. Workman made extensive alterations to the house in 1869, in a style reminiscent of manor houses in his native England.

La Casa Nueva
1919–23

Built by Workman's grandson, Walter P. Temple, this two-story Spanish Colonial Revival house contains some exceptional stained glass, wood carving and iron work. A dominant feature is the stained-glass window above the main staircase, which depicts the landing of the Spanish in California. Completely restored and furnished in the 1920s style, the house contains some original family pieces.

El Campo Santo

A tree-lined walk connects the Workman and Temple residences with an acre of land that John Workman set aside in 1850 as the family burial ground. Its Greek Revival mausoleum contains the remains of the last governor of Mexican California, Pio Pico, and his wife Ygnacia.

Workman and Temple Homestead, 15415 East Don Julian Road, City of Industry, CA 91744; (213) 968-8492
Hours: 1–4 Tuesday-Friday, 10–4 on the first and third weekends of each month

(Courtesy of the Workman and Temple Homestead)

Pomona

Adobe de Palomares
1854

The thirteen-room, T-shaped adobe with the shake roof that stands beside the road once called Camino de San Bernardino was the second home constructed by Ygnacio Palomares on the Rancho San Jose, which was granted to him and Ricardo Viejar in 1837. A busy stage station and a popular tavern in Don Ygnacio's day, the adobe has since been restored and refurnished in the style of the period. Many of the furnishings are heirlooms donated or loaned by descendants of early families. The gardens have also been restored, and are as close as possible to their original form and beauty.

Adobe de Palomares, 491 East Arrow Highway, Pomona, CA 91767; (714) 620-2300
Hours: 2–5 daily except Monday; closed Thanksgiving, Christmas and New Year's days

(Courtesy of the Historical Society of Pomona Valley, Inc.)

Adobe de Palomares (below)

Pomona

La Casa Primera
1837; altered 1867

La Casa Primera is the Pomona Valley's oldest home; it was built by Ygnacio Palomares on the Rancho San Jose, which was granted to him and Ricardo Viejar in the early 1830s. After occupying the adobe for seventeen years, Don Ygnacio and his family moved to the newly constructed Adobe de Palomares, about a mile farther north. It was not until 1867 that Don Ygna- cio's son, Francisco Palomares, restored the older house; Francisco then lived there with his wife Lujardo Alvarado until his death in 1882. Today the adobe is furnished with authentic 1837 pieces. It stands in an old-fashioned garden that still features orange trees planted by Don Francisco more than a century ago.

La Casa Primera, 1569 *North Park Avenue, Pomona, CA 91768*
Hours: 2–5 Sunday

(*Courtesy of the Historical Society of Pomona Valley, Inc.*)

Pomona

Phillips Mansion
1875

Formerly surrounded by broad ranch lands, this dignified post–Civil War mansion built for Louis Phillips was the first brick residence constructed in Pomona Valley. It passed from the Phillips family's ownership in 1930 and was destined for demolition before being purchased by the Historical Society of Pomona Valley in 1966. The society has refurbished the mansion to its original beauty, designating some of the rooms as memorials to pioneer families of the valley. The Victorian furnishings include some original Phillips pieces.

Phillips Mansion, 2640 Pomona Boulevard, Pomona, CA 91768
Hours: 2–5 *the first Sunday of each month*

(Courtesy of the Historical Society of Pomona Valley, Inc.)

Whittier

Jonathan Bailey Home
ca. 1868

The town of Whittier could be said to have grown up around the Jonathan Bailey Home. It was from this small frame ranch house, where "Uncle" Jonathan Bailey and his wife lived between 1887 and 1894, that Bailey directed the development of the fledgling Quaker community. The town's first religious service was conducted on the porch four days after the Baileys moved in, and their home continued to serve as a meeting house until a church was built.

The house predates the founding of Whittier by several years. Although its exact age is not known, it is probably more than a century old; a German immigrant, Jacob Gerkins, is known to have homesteaded the property in 1868. The Bailey Home is now shown with furnishings of the period 1880–1900, and the gardens have been restored with plants popular at that time.

Jonathan Bailey Home, 13421 *East Camilla Street, Whittier, CA 90605*
Hours: 1–3 *Wednesday and Sunday*
Admission by donation

(*Courtesy of the Whittier Historical Society and Friends of the Bailey House*)

Whittier

Pio Pico State Historic Park
1852

In its heyday, the favorite home of Pio Pico—the last governor of Mexican California—was a considerable mansion, and it was surrounded by the 9,000-acre Rancho Paso de Bartolo Viejo. Forming a U about a spacious patio and garden, the building stood two stories high, with adobe walls, a gabled roof, thirty-three handsomely appointed rooms and—rare for the time—wooden flooring and fireplaces. Here Pico and his wife, Dona Maria Ygnacia Alvarado, lived in luxurious style.

Toward the end of Pico's life, however, this halcyon period ended. In 1883 the San Gabriel River overran its banks, destroying almost half the mansion. Pico unwisely put up all his properties as security for a loan for rebuilding. On the due date, he could not meet his obligation; by taking the case to court he staved off settlement, but ultimately, in 1892, the California Supreme Court ruled against him. Virtually penniless, Pico then lived on the charity of friends and relatives in Los Angeles until his death two years later. He is buried at Rancho La Puente (at what is now the Workman and Temple Homestead in City of Industry, California).

Nine of the thirteen rooms that remain of the Pio Pico Mansion have been restored and furnished as for the period 1850–90. Among the items are a few that belonged to Pico himself.

Pio Pico State Historic Park, 6003 *Pioneer Boulevard, Whittier, CA 90606; (213) 695-1217*
Hours: 10–4 Tuesday-Sunday
Admission fee

(*Courtesy of the California Department of Parks and Recreation and the Whittier Historical Society*)

Riverside & San Bernardino Counties

Chino

Yorba-Slaughter Adobe 1850–56

Considered a good example of early-California adobe construction, this single-story ranch house built with Indian labor by Bernardo Yorba for his son Raimundo was a relay station for the famous Butterfield stages. It was purchased in 1868 by a Mexican War veteran, Fenton Slaughter, who, with ten children to house, enclosed the porch on the south and west sides to double the number of rooms. From his death in 1897 until its restoration in 1928 (by Julia Fenton Fugua, as a memorial to her father), the adobe served as a chicken house and mushroom farm. It is now owned and maintained by San Bernardino County as a museum of the Mexican rancho period, furnished in large part with pieces purchased in Boston by the Slaughters and shipped 'round the Horn. A notable item from the days when California's economy depended on cattle and hides is the huge tallow-rendering pot, made of solid copper in Spain 160 years ago. It weighs one ton.

Yorba-Slaughter Adobe, 17127 Pomona
  Rincon Road, Chino, CA 91710; (714)
  597-2611
*Hours: Daylight saving time, 10–5 Saturday
  and 1–5 Sunday; Standard time, 10–4:30
  Saturday and 12:30–4:30 Sunday
Admission by donation*

(Courtesy of the San Bernardino County Museum)

Death Valley

Scotty's Castle
1925–31
Death Valley National Monument

Improbable as the tales told by "Death Valley Scotty," Scotty's Castle rises abruptly from the floor of a side canyon at the northern end of Death Valley National Monument. This ornate, Mediterranean-style structure, combining elements of Spanish, Moorish and Italian architecture, was built by insurance millionaire Albert Mussey Johnson. Johnson lavished an estimated $2 million on transforming a handful of existing ranch buildings into an extraordinary vacation retreat, complete with a carillon tower, an organ, and a stream running through the castle yard. Even so, he was not able to complete the nine-building complex as planned; in the stock-market crash of 1929 he lost much of his fortune.

Purchased by the National Park Service in 1970, the castle is maintained as it was when the Johnsons lived there. The original massive furniture is still in place, as are the unusual, hand-painted sheepskin draperies and the gun collection assembled by Johnson and Scotty. The interiors are richly ornamented.

That the home has come to be called Scotty's Castle is a testament to the creative tongue and flamboyant personality of Mr. and Mrs. Johnson's friend Walter Scott, known as Death Valley Scotty. A former Buffalo Bill Cody show rider and pseudoprospector, Scotty beguiled the national press for fifty years with his stunts. He was largely financed by the tolerant Johnson, who once explained that "Scotty repays me in laughs."

Scotty's Castle, Grapevine Canyon, Death Valley National Monument, CA 92328; (714) 786-2331

Hours: By guided tour only, 9–5 daily. Because winter-month tours often sell out by noon, the best times to visit Scotty's Castle are late spring (May–June) and early fall (September–October).

Admission fee

(Courtesy of the National Park Service)

Rancho Cucamonga

John Rains House
1860

San Bernardino County's first fired-brick building stands on land that was part of the Rancho Cucamonga granted to Tiburcio Tapia in 1839. In 1856 the ranch was purchased by John Rains, a cattleman and vineyardist. By marrying Maria Merced Williams, heiress of the Chino Rancho and granddaughter of Don Antonio Lugo, Rains allied himself to one of the region's most prominent families. Rains and his wife built a square, single-story home with a central courtyard open to the sky; features such as the central breezeway, white trim around the windows and high ceilings hint that Rains may have looked to the plantation houses of his native South for inspiration. He was not to enjoy his new home long; in November 1862 he was murdered on his way to Los Angeles, for reasons that were never determined and by people whose identities were never learned.

The house changed hands a number of times before it was saved from the wrecker's ball and restored, in the 1970s. Today it is a satellite museum of the San Bernardino County Museum and is furnished in the style of the 1860s and 1870s. The grounds are gradually being replanted with trees and with roses popular during the Rainses' occupancy.

John Rains House, 8810 Hemlock Avenue, Rancho Cucamonga, CA 91730; (714) 989-4970
Hours: 12–4 Wednesday-Sunday

(Courtesy of the Casa de Rancho Cucamonga Historical Society)

Redlands

Kimberly Crest
1897

Flanked by terraced gardens, Kimberly Crest sits proudly on a hill top affording a splendid panorama of Redlands Valley and the San Bernardino Mountains. This elegant essay in the style of a sixteenth century French chateau, with steep roofs, dormer windows and round towers capped by large decorative finials, was built by Mrs. Cornelia Hill of New York State. In 1905 it was purchased by John Alfred Kimberly, one of the founders of the Kimberly-Clark Corporation, and the home remained in his family until 1979.

The spacious interior is marked by highly polished woodwork, by a great hall with a minstrel's gallery, and by a painted parlor installed by Tiffany's. Furnishings throughout are family pieces, including European antiques and family mememtos.

Kimberly Crest, *1325 Prospect Drive, Redlands, CA 92373; (714) 792-2111*
Hours: 1–4 Thursday and the first Sunday of each month; closed legal holidays and in January and August
Admission fee

(Courtesy of the Kimberly-Shirk Association)

Redlands

The Morey Mansion
1890

Such varied elements as a Saracenic onion dome, Gothic and Romanesque arched windows, a French mansard roof, Italianate balustrades and a Chinese-tracery veranda are deftly combined in this splendid two-story Queen Anne mansion. Built by retired shipbuilder David Morey with the earnings of his wife's tree farm, the twenty-room house contains a wealth of fine carving that enhances the golden oak woodwork used in the interior. Nautical touches abound. The vestibule features a paneled Union Jack, the reception-hall paneling is reminiscent of a ship's cabin's, anchors appear among the fruits and flowers of the carv-ing, and the onion dome was constructed in the manner of a ship's prow. Notable, too, is the Tiffany-style stained glass used in some of the transoms and the cast bronze hardware.

If the Morey Mansion seems familiar, there is good reason. Although now a private home, it has appeared in movies, on television and in many advertisements, as well as in books and magazines. Current owners Carl Ljungquist and Gary Conway have completely restored the mansion and its outbuildings, and the two-acre garden will be relandscaped.

The Morey Mansion, 190 *Terracina Boulevard, Redlands, CA 92373. For tour information, call the YWCA; (714) 793-2957 Hours: 1–5 the first Sunday of each month Admission fee*

(Courtesy of Carl E. Ljungquist and Gary M. Conway)

Riverside

Heritage House
1891

Queen Anne, Moorish, Georgian and Chinese features are impressively combined in this two-story mansion built by Mrs. Catherine Bettner, widow of a prominent Riverside land developer. It was one of the first homes in the area to have gas lighting, which was powered by a gas generator in the back yard; many of the original fixtures, remodeled and converted to electricity in 1906, are still in place. In 1969 Heritage House was purchased by the city of Riverside and restored. A number of the original Bettner pieces are among the furnishings, which largely reflect the period 1891–1900. Restoration of the gardens and carriage house to the style of the same period is in progress.

Heritage House,8193 *Magnolia Avenue,*
Riverside, CA 92501; (714) 689-1333
Hours: 12–2:30 Tuesday and Thursday,
12–3:30 Sunday; closed July and August

(Courtesy of the City of Riverside Municipal Museum)

Yucaipa

Sepulveda Adobe
1841–1843

San Bernadino County's oldest building is a typical early-California two-story adobe ranch house, with a covered veranda running the length of the front facade. Built by Diego Sepulveda on land that had belonged to Mission San Gabriel, it was purchased by Mormon colonists in 1851 and sold by them to a former mountain man, James Waters, in 1857. In 1869 Waters in turn sold the adobe and 4,000 acres to a Texas cattleman, John Dunlap, whose family retained possession until 1954. The rooms that are open to the public contain furnishings of the Sepulveda family brought from Spain around Cape Horn in 1802, as well as late-nineteenth-century pieces owned by the Dunlaps.

Sepulveda Adobe, 32183 *Kentucky Street,*
Yucaipa, CA 92399; (714) 795–7507
Hours: 10–5 Tuesday–Saturday, 12–5 Sunday

(Courtesy of the San Bernardino County Museum)

San Joaquin Valley

Bakersfield

Guild House
1905

This turn-of-the-century home with Queen Anne detailing now houses a restaurant and art gallery whose proceeds benefit Valley Guild projects. It contains period furniture, Tiffany light fixtures and a marble fireplace purchased from Gumps in San Francisco in 1905.

Guild House, *1905 Eighteenth Street, Bakersfield, CA 93301; (805) 325-5478*
Hours: Gallery, 9:30–3:30 Monday–Friday; restaurant, 12–2 Monday–Friday; closed mid-June until mid-September

(Courtesy of the Valley Guild, Inc.)

Bakersfield

Kern County Museum Pioneer Village

The Kern County Museum has assembled more than thirty-five early buildings on a fifteen-acre tract behind the main exhibit hall to recreate a Kern County frontier community of the pioneer era. The most notable residences are:

Weill House
1882

The Alphonse Weill home, often called Bakersfield's first "modern" house, boasts an elegant interior with a living-room fireplace of simulated carved stone and twelve-foot-high ceilings to allow air circulation during Bakersfield's extremely hot summer. It also still has most of its original furnishings. An interesting feature is the lack of a kitchen in the home; meals were prepared in a separate cookhouse. The home was occupied by the Weill family until 1949, when it was brought to Pioneer Village.

Weill House (below)

Barnes Log Cabin
1868

Freighter Thomas Barnes built this sturdy cabin on the Canfield Ranch, with cedar and pine logs washed downstream in the Kern River floods of 1867. It contains furnishings of the period and features a large fireplace that served the kitchen and served also as a central heating system.

W. A. Howell House
1891

This fine example of the Queen Anne style is characterized by high ceilings, double doors, porches and stained-glass windows. It has speaking tubes for upstairs-downstairs communication and the the turn-of-the-century kitchen is equipped with both electric and gas lighting. Originally located on the corner of Seventeenth and H streets in Bakersfield, the house was brought to the museum in 1969. Most of the furnishings were donated by the Howell family.

Barnes Log Cabin (below)

W.A. Howell House (opposite)

Weller Ranch
ca. 1890

Surrounded by appropriate outbuildings at the Bakersfield site, the single-story Weller ranch house actually was built in Rosedale, by an English "remittance man." It typifies California ranch architecture between 1875 and 1915.

Metcalf House
1885

Built by Thomas Metcalf for his daughter Maude, a pioneer Bakersfield school teacher, this pleasant single-story frame house is typical of tract homes put up in the 1880s. Its furnishings, although not original to the house, are characteristic of the period.

Kern County Museum Pioneer Village, 3801 Chester Avenue, Bakersfield, CA 93301; (805) 861-2132
Hours: 8–3:30 Monday–Friday, 10–3:30 Saturday, Sunday and holidays; closed Thanksgiving, Christmas and New Year's days
Admission fee

(Courtesy of the Kern County Museum)

Fresno

Kearney Mansion
1901

In 1901 Martin Theodore Kearney—real estate baron, raisin grower and agriculture promoter—built this French Renaissance mansion as temporary quarters. He planned an even grander mansion that would be modeled on the Château Chenonceaux, but it was never built. Kearney Mansion is now the home and museum of the Fresno City and County Historical Society, which has restored it as closely as possible to its appearance in Kearney's day. The house retains much of its original decor and approximately half of the original furnishings. Particularly notable are the scenic French wallpapers commissioned by Kearney and the hand-carved Black Forest oak furniture he purchased in Germany.

Tours include a second building as well; the servants quarters (ca. 1890), with a kitchen where two Chinese cooks and their helpers prepared meals for Kearney's workers, as many as two hundred men at a time. This building, Kearney's first home on the property, also features two special-collections rooms with changing historic exhibits.

Kearney Mansion, *7160 West Kearney Boulevard, Fresno, CA 93706; (209) 441-0862*
Hours: January and February, 1–4 Saturday and Sunday; March–December, 1–4 Thursday–Sunday; closed Thanksgiving, Christmas and New Year's days
Admission fee

(Courtesy of the Fresno City and County Historical Society)

Fresno

Meux Home
1888–89

Sole survivor among the large Victorian homes constructed during Fresno's first twenty years, this two-story house with a large, roofed porch and a peaked tower was built by a former Confederate surgeon and pioneer Fresno physician, Thomas R. Meux. A variety of textures and decoration—horizontal clapboards, fish-scale shingles and floral relief work—mark the exterior. Of particular interest are the spindle-work porch columns and the octagonal master bedroom. The Meux Home, occupied by the family until 1970, has been restored and refurnished with items dating from 1880 to approximately 1920, with a view to portraying the lifestyle of an upper-middle-class family of early Fresno. Memorabilia of the Meux family are displayed, and one room contains the Shoup Collection of turn-of-the-century toys and dolls.

Meux Home, *Tulare and R streets, Fresno, CA 93707; (209) 233-8007*
Hours: 12–4 Thursday–Sunday
Admission fee

(Courtesy of the Meux Home Museum Corporation)

Lompoc

Fabing-McKay-Spanne House
1875

Lompoc Valley's first two-story frame house was built for Henry Wadsworth Fabing, a onetime blacksmith from New York State who later turned to farming and carriage making. For the construction, redwood was brought by steamship to Point Sal, floated ashore and dragged by horse teams to Lompoc. The structure's name refers to other owners as well in its history. Now headquarters of the Lompoc Valley Historical Society, the house has been furnished with some of the pieces originally belonging to early owners.

Fabing-McKay-Spanne House, 207 North "L" Street, Lompoc, CA 93436; (805) 736-5044
Hours: 2–5 on the fourth Sunday of each month and by appointment
Admission by donation

(Courtesy of the Lompoc Valley Historical Society, Inc.)

Porterville

Zalud House
1891

In 1891 Czech-born John Zalud capped his progress from twenty-eight-dollar-a-month muleteer for New Orleans's streetcar company to prosperous restaurateur and rancher by building a substantial home. He constructed it of brick with a mansard roof, and it was never remodeled; it is shown with most of its original furnishings and with memorabilia of the Zalud family. The remarkably beautiful garden still has several of the roses planted before 1900.

Zalud House, *393 Hockett Street, Porterville, CA 93257; (209) 784-1400, ext. 444 Hours: 10–4 Wednesday-Saturday, 2–4 Sunday Admission fee*

(Courtesy of the City of Porterville Parks and Leisure Services Department)

Zalud House (below)

Orange & San Diego Counties

Anaheim

Mother Colony House
1857–58

One of the first houses to go up in the experimental colony founded by German settlers at Anaheim in 1857 was this small, redwood frame cottage consisting of two or three rooms and a sheltering porch across the front. It served as the home and business office of George Hansen, general manager during the colony's early years, and it retains much of its original woodwork, including the redwood floors installed in 1857.

After Hansen sold the house, in 1863, it passed through several hands; it was moved to its present site when deeded to the Daughters of the American Revolution. Now the property of the city of Anaheim, the Mother Colony House displays furniture, clothing and household items donated by descendants of Anaheim's pioneer families. The attractive gardens include a grape arbor with the same variety of mission grapes planted by George Hansen in 1857.

Mother Colony House, 414 North West Street, Anaheim, CA 92805; (714) 999-1850
Hours: Wednesday, 3–5, 1:30–4 Sunday

(Courtesy of the City of Anaheim Public Library)

Norwalk

Gilbert Sproul House
1870

Norwalk's founder, Gilbert Sproul, built this simple redwood home with few pretensions to architectural style. An adventurous Yankee from Maine, Sproul had traveled widely in the West Indies and the Orient before settling down as a lumber baron in Oregon; he also was quick to sense the opportunities when Southern California's great ranchos were subdivided and settlers poured into the state. His house became the scene of many of Norwalk's early town meetings. Donated with all its original furnishings to the city by Sproul's granddaughter in 1964, it is now a museum furnished with contemporary antiques.

Gilbert Sproul House, *12237 Sproul Street, Norwalk, CA 90650; (213) 864-9663*
Hours: 10–2 Wednesday–Friday, 12–5 Saturday and Sunday

(Courtesy of the Gilbert Sproul Museum)

Norwalk

Hargitt House Museum
1891

D. D. Johnston, organizer of Norwalk's first school system, built this handsome two-story house with ornate bargeboards. It became the property of the city in 1975, at the death of Johnston's grandson, and now is shown with its original furnishings.

Hargitt House Museum, *12450 Mapledale Avenue, Norwalk, CA 90650; (213) 864-9663*
Hours: 1–4 Saturday and Sunday

(Courtesy of the Gilbert Sproul Museum)

San Diego

Old Town San Diego State Historic Park

The adobes of Old Town State Historic Park are a link to the time when San Diego changed its character to that of a town rather than a military-religious outpost in the wilderness. Since 1769 life had centered on the mission and the presidio, but in the 1820s a plaza was laid out to form the nucleus of a settlement now called "Old Town." By the 1830s about forty houses lined the streets, four of which still stand today, in the park. Two home have been restored much as their builders knew them and are open to the public.

La Casa de Estudillo
1827

On the east side of the plaza is a large U-shaped, single-story adobe, its slanting tile roof surmounted by a cupola. This, the most famous of Old Town's original adobes, was built by Capt. Jose Maria de Estudillo, commander of the San Diego presidio. During his lifetime it was a brilliant center of social life in California from San Diego to Monterey. The casa's twelve rooms and chapel open onto a spacious patio with native California plantings. Of interest in the construction of the house is the use of leather thongs to bind together the massive beams that support the roof. The furnishings are not original but have been assembled by the Colonial Dames of America, who attempted to determine exactly what the Estudillos had ordered from Europe.

La Casa Machado y Stewart
1830s

This simple two-room structure was one of four or five adobes built much alike by Don Jose Manuel Machado for himself and his married daughters. It was the home of one Richard Henry Dana's shipmates; Jack Stewart, a Yankee from Maine, served in the U.S. Army and then became a pilot on San Diego Bay, marrying Machado's youngest daughter in 1845. Occupied by their descendants until 1966, the casa is furnished with antiques appropriate to the period.

Old Town San Diego State Historic Park,
San Diego, CA 92110; (714) 237-6770
Hours: Summer, 10–6 daily; winter, 10–5 daily;
   daily tour at 2; closed Thanksgiving, Christmas
   and New Year's days
Admission fee

(Courtesy of the California Department of Parks and Recreation)

San Diego

Derby-Pendleton House
1851

Built in 1851 in Portland, Maine, this small Greek Revival house was disassembled, shipped 'round the Horn to San Diego, reassembled and given by Juan Bandini to his daughter and Capt. Charles Johnson as a wedding gift. It was later occupied by Lt. George H. Derby, the U.S. Army engineer who redirected the course of the San Diego River, and by Capt. George Pendleton, a county clerk.

Derby-Pendleton House, 1962 *Harney Street, San Diego, CA 92110*
Hours: 10–4:30 Wednesday–Sunday

(Courtesy of the Historical Shrine Foundation of San Diego County)

San Diego

Villa Montezuma
(Jesse Shepard House)
1887

Boldly hued and striking of outline, Jesse Shepard's home on the slopes of Gold Hill is a splendid monument to San Diego's boom years of the 1880s. The two-story mansion, vaguely Queen Anne in style with its domed tower, turrets, gables, ornate detailing and variegated shingles, was more the design of Shepard than of the architects (Comstock and Trotsche) he commissioned. Shepard designed the art-glass windows fabricated in San Francisco, selected the fabrics and furnishings, and achieved a rich interior with his skillful use of polished redwood walls offset by silvery Lincrusta-Walton ceilings.

At this home Shepard, who had gained international renown as a concert pianist, began to write professionally, using the pen name Frances Grierson. In 1889 he left San Diego to follow a literary career in Europe; he died in obscurity in Los Angeles in 1927. Restored and furnished with period antiques, Villa Montezuma today is maintained as a historic house museum and cultural center by the San Diego Historical Society.

Villa Montezuma, 1925 *K Street, San Diego, CA 92102; (714) 239-2211*
Hours: 1–4:30 Tuesday–Friday, 1–4:30 Sunday
Admission by donation

(Courtesy of the San Diego Historical Society)

San Diego

Whaley House
1856

When Thomas Whaley, an energetic and talented New York businessman, arrived in San Diego after two years in San Francisco, he saw in the dusty little pioneer town with the splendid bay and Italian climate the same possibilities as New York's. By 1856 he had turned sufficient profit to begin construction of a two-story building that would serve as a house and a store. Using bricks from his own yard at La Playa, he built what is believed to be the oldest brick structure in Southern California, pleasingly proportioned and in the Greek Revival style. Variously used as a granary, Sunday school, social center and theater, the Whaley home also served as the county courthouse from 1869 until 1871. It was occupied as a home until 1953, when Corinne Lillian Whaley, the youngest of Thomas's six children, died at the age of eighty-nine.

After years of neglect, the Whaley House has been fully restored and furnished with items of the 1850s and 1860s from other early San Diego homes. It is also reputed to contain a number of intangible assets: the several Whaley House ghosts, seen, heard and sensed by many, have been the subject of several investigations. Thus it may be that a gentleman come upon in frock coat and pantaloons on the upper landing is not a costumed docent. . . .

Whaley House, 2482 San Diego Avenue, San Diego, CA 92110; (714) 298-2482
Hours: 10–4:30 daily
Admission fee

(Courtesy of the Historical Shrine Foundation of San Diego County)

Whaley House (below)

Spring Valley

Bancroft Ranch House Museum
1863

Historian and publisher Hubert Howe Bancroft wrote part of his celebrated *History of California* in this unpretentious adobe ranch house, which he purchased in 1885 as his retirement home. Built by Judge Augustus S. Ensworth, this house, the first to be constructed by a white man in what is now Spring Valley, incorporates timbers salvaged from a sailing vessel that ran aground in San Diego Bay. It is now a museum of local history.

Bancroft Ranch House Museum, 9050 Memory Lane, Spring Valley, CA 92077; (714) 469-1480
Hours: 1–4 Wednesday–Sunday

(Courtesy of the Spring Valley Historical Society)

Bancroft Ranch House Museum (below)

Index